The Presence
on the Spirit

The Presence of the Dead on the Spiritual Path

Seven Lectures
Held in Various Cities Between
April 17 and May 26, 1914

Translated by
Christian von Arnim

Edited by
Joachim Reuter

ANTHROPOSOPHIC PRESS

This book is a translation of *Wie erwirbt man sich Verständnis für die geistige Welt?* (volume 154 in the Collected Works), published by Rudolf Steiner Verlag, Dornach, Switzerland, 1985.

Published in the United States by Anthroposophic Press, Bells Pond, Star Route, Hudson, New York 12534.

Library of Congress Cataloging-in-Publication Data

Steiner, Rudolf, 1861-1925
[Wie erwirbt man sich Verständnis für die geistige Welt? English]
The presence of the dead on the spiritual path : seven lectures held in various cities between April 17 and May 26, 1914 /Rudolf Steiner : translated by Christian von Arnim ; edited by Joachim Reuter.
p. cm.
Translation of: Wie Erwirbt man sich Verstädnis für die geistige Welt?
ISBN 0-88010-282-9 — ISBN 0-88010-283-7 (pbk.)
1. Spiritualism. I. Reuter, Joachim. II. Title.
BP595.S894W4413 1990
299'.935—dc20 90-33836
CIP

10 9 8 7 6 5 4 3 2

Book design and Typography by Studio 31/Royal Type

Printed in the United States of America

CONTENTS

LECTURE ONE

UNDERSTANDING THE SPIRITUAL WORLD

(PART ONE)

Berlin, April 18, 1914

When you remember a dream, it will probably be quite obvious to you that during the dream you merely observed the images weaving before your soul without having a clear awareness of yourself. Self-awareness, then, is not as clear in dreaming as it is in waking consciousness. The images weaving before the soul present two types of scenes. There are either series of images familiar to the dreamer because they relate to recent or not-so-recent events, or scenes where such events are changed in all sorts of ways, their form altered to such an extent that specific occurrences are unrecognizable, and we think we are dreaming of something completely new. We can indeed have dreams that are not connected with any experiences we have had and are therefore completely new. But in each case, we will have had a feeling that a type of living, weaving image has been revealed to the soul. This is what we remember after waking up. Some dreams remain in our memory longer and others seem to vanish as soon as we have to deal with the events of the day.

So today let us examine what we perceive in such weaving dreams. We know what we perceive when we are awake in this world, which we call the physical. But what fills our perception when we dream, as events and material things fill our daytime experience? It is what we call the etheric world, the etheric substance permeating the world with its inner processes and with all that lives in it. That is the essence, as it were, of our perceptions when we dream. But we usually perceive only a very small part of the etheric world when dreaming. The etheric world is inaccessible to us when we are awake and perceive the physical realm; we cannot perceive the etheric substance around us with our physical senses. Likewise we cannot perceive all of it in our ordinary dreams, but only a part of it, namely, our own etheric body.

As you know, we leave our physical and our etheric bodies behind in sleep. In our usual dreams we look back, as it were, from within our astral body and I to what we have left behind in sleep. However, we are then not aware of our physical body and do not use our physical senses. Rather, we look back only at our etheric body. Fundamentally, therefore, processes in our etheric body reveal themselves in certain places, and we perceive them as dreams. In fact, most dreams are nothing else but looking at our etheric body in sleep and becoming aware of some of its exceedingly complex processes.

Our etheric body is very complex and contains all our memories, ready to present them to us when we recall them. Even those things that have sunk down into the depths of the soul, things we are not aware of in waking consciousness, are contained in the etheric body in some way. Our whole life in this incarnation is retained in the etheric body, is really present in it. Of course, this is very difficult to imagine, but it is true nevertheless. Imagine you were to talk all day long, as some people do, and everything you said was recorded on records. When the first record is full, you take a second one, then a third, and so on. The number of records would depend on how much you spoke. Now if someone collected all the records, everything you had said would be nicely preserved on records at the end of the day. Then, if someone played them, everything you said during the day would be heard again. In a similar way, all our memories are retained in the etheric body. Under the special conditions of sleep one part of the etheric body appears before us, as though—to stay with this metaphor—we took one record from the collection and played it; this is the most common kind of dream. Thus our consciousness weaves in our own etheric body.

The same applies to hallucinations affecting our soul. As a rule, such hallucinations arise because the person can see with the ego and the astral body, which are still in the physical body, a section of the etheric body that has become detached. This can happen when a part of your physical body is ill, the nervous system, for example. Your etheric body is then unable to penetrate the physical at the point where the nervous system is diseased; it is cast out there, so to speak. The etheric body itself is not sick, but it has been separated from the physical body in a specific place. If it could remain in the physical body, our normal state of consciousness would prevail, and we would be unaware that our physical body is sick. When the part our etheric body cannot penetrate shines out toward it, we experience this in our consciousness as a hallucination.

This etheric substance, from which dreams or hallucinations develop, surrounds us everywhere in the world. And our own etheric body is like a section that has been cut out of this etheric substance. After passing through the gate of death and discarding our physical body, we pass through this etheric substance and never really leave it on our path between death and a new birth. It is everywhere and we have to pass through it; we are in it. Sometime after death, we discard our etheric body, which dissolves into this surrounding etheric substance. Usually, we cannot perceive this outer etheric substance. That is why we have nothing in the etheric world that could be called perception, parallel to perception in the physical world. Our perceptions of the etheric in our dreams depend completely on us.

True perception of the etheric world after death or here on earth in clairvoyant Imaginations requires greater strength than we usually have between birth and death. We need greater inner strength of soul. We do not perceive the etheric world around us during earthly life because we lack sufficient strength of soul. To perceive the etheric world we must become much more active, work much harder than we do in ordinary life. After death, too, the soul must be filled with much more active strength than in ordinary life to relate to its environment. Otherwise we do not perceive the etheric world, just as we wouldn't perceive anything if we lacked all senses in the physical world. Thus, we need a more active strength of soul to find our way after death and not to be deaf and blind, figuratively speaking, to the world we enter then.

To get a clearer idea of how the soul perceives after death, or after it has developed the faculties to unfold its imagination, let us compare this soul faculty to writing. What you write down expresses something that stands behind your words; still, it is you who put down the letters. You have the power to make what you write true, to make it correspond to an objective state of affairs. If you want to inform a faraway friend about something and write it down for him, it is you who form the words that will tell the friend about the fact when he reads them. Someone may object that this fact does not exist in the world as an objective fact, but is only what someone has written down. This is nonsense, of course. It is possible to describe an objective fact with the letters you wrote. The same applies to imaginative perception in the supersensible world. You have to be active. You have to set down the signs, the letters that express the objective processes in the spiritual world, and you must be aware that this is what you are doing. Whether you can do that or not depends on whether you have the strength necessary for a living relationship with spiritual reality, whether it inspires you to set down the truth and not falsehoods. But the fact remains: You have to know you are setting it down.

Now, let us return to dreams. When we dream, we usually feel the dream images "weave" and simply unravel on their own. We should think of these dreams as images that float past the soul. Now suppose you were thinking that you yourself place the dream images in space and time just as you set down letters on paper. This is not what we normally associate with dreams or hallucinations, but it is the type of consciousness required for imaginative thinking. You must be aware that you are the determining power in your dreams. You put down one thing after another just as you do when writing something on paper. You yourself are in control. The same power is behind you that makes what you write true. The great difference between dreams or hallucinations and true clairvoyance is that in the latter we are aware that we are the esoteric scribes, as it were. The things we see are noted down as an esoteric script. We inscribe onto the world what we perceive as expression, as revelation, of the world.

Here, people could object that we do not need to write these things down because they are known beforehand. But that is not valid, for in this case it is not we who do the writing but the being of the next higher hierarchy. We give ourselves up to that being, and it becomes the force ruling us. In an inner soul process, we record what holds sway through us. When you look at this esoteric script, you will read what is to be revealed.

That is why I have said so often in public lectures that the development of clairvoyance requires that all perception becomes active and does not remain the passive openness to the world that is appropriate for understanding our physical environment. Gradually, then, we comprehend what we have called "learning the esoteric script," since the beginning of our anthroposophic work. I have described it in more detail in *The Threshold of the Spiritual World.*[1] To write the esoteric script into spiritual space and spiritual time our soul must be more active and powerful than it needs to be in everyday life. We need this greater strength when we have passed through the gate of death. If you seek imaginative clairvoyance, you will achieve it gradually through meditation. You will experience and perceive, knowing all the while you are in a world of which our dreams are but a weak reflection. You can live in that world in such a way that you can control your dreams, just as you are in control when you assemble a table or a shoe.

Many people object they have tried to meditate in all kinds of ways but are still not becoming clairvoyant. This lack of clairvoyance simply shows they do not really want the activity and strength I have just described. They consider themselves fortunate because they do not need them. They do not *want* to develop any active strength of soul, but want to become clairvoyant without having to acquire this strength first. They want the tableau that arises before them through clairvoyance to appear by itself. But that would be nothing but hallucinating or dreaming. To put it bluntly, a dream is a piece of the etheric world that we can take with our etheric feelers and move from one place to another. This has nothing to do with true clairvoyance. In experiencing true second sight we are as active as we are in the physical world in writing on paper. The only difference is that when we want to write in the physical world, we need first to know what it is we want to write down — at least it usually helps if we do. By contrast, in spiritual perception we allow the beings of the spiritual hierarchies to write, and only then, while we are writing, do the things appear that we are to perceive. Real clairvoyance cannot come about without our active involvement in every single aspect of our perception.

We also need the strength that enables us to write in the etheric world when we have passed through the gate of death. The kind of thinking that serves us well in the physical world is of no use for perception after death. A person may be exceedingly clever and smart about things of the physical world, but after death these capacities will be of no help. This kind of thinking is much too weak for writing anything into the etheric world. All ideas we have developed relating to physical things have their origin in this weak thinking, which is useless after death. We need a stronger kind of thinking, one that is inwardly active of its own accord. We need thinking that forms thoughts which do not merely mirror the outer sense world. We must develop this inner capacity to form thoughts independent of anything external that arise, as it were, from the depths of the soul, or we cannot have a corresponding capacity after death.

Now you might object that we could just think up all kinds of things, or create a lot of fantasies that do not reflect anything external, and then we would be well prepared for developing the strength of thinking necessary after death. It could be that someone wants to have a great deal of thinking ability after death and therefore imagines winged dragons, which do not exist, terrifying beasts, and so on. The person imagines all these things so as not to be tied to the apron strings of outer images, and to be able to develop inner strength of thinking in preparation for life after death.

It cannot be denied — people who do this will have greater faculties in the world after death than those who do not. However, they would perceive only false images, distortions, just as people with impaired vision see a distorted image of the physical world and those with damaged hearing have a false impression of its sounds. People who follow this course of action sentence themselves to perceiving nothing but grotesque things in the etheric world, instead of what is truly rooted there.

In past periods of human development, care was always taken to ensure that human beings were given mental images neither borrowed from the physical world nor created in the arbitrary and fantastical manner I have just described. According to the methods available to them, the great founders of our religions handed down images not based on the physical, but on the spiritual world. Thus, by following their religious teachers, people were able to develop mental images that were not tied to the sensory world but were true all the same because they originated in the spiritual world. This is the immensely great education of the human race undertaken by the founders of our religions. They had set themselves the task of giving human beings images that would help them to develop a kind of thinking that would keep them from arriving spiritually deaf and blind in the spiritual world after death. The founders of our religions wanted to be certain that human beings were fully alive, fully conscious, and that their consciousness would not vanish or fade in their hour of death or become a false consciousness then.

As I have often said, we are currently living at a stage of evolution when human beings are meant to come of age, as it were. Religious founders will no longer appear as they formerly did and appeal to our faith. Those times are past, although, of course, they still reach into our time. At present, only a few people are beginning to experience this new existence, so to speak. Most still yearn to cling to the traditional ideas of the ancient founders of religions. But humanity must come of age and what the founders of religions provided for our faith must be replaced by the contribution of modern spiritual science. For this science of the spirit is by nature completely different from those ancient teachings. In order to avoid misunderstandings, we must emphasize that when we speak of the old religious founders we are not including Christ among them. I have often said that Christ's significance does not lie in his teachings, but in what took place through him. The ancient religious founders were in a sense teachers, but Christ's main deed was to imbue humanity with His own power through the Mystery of Golgotha. To this day, this has been extremely difficult for many people to understand. That is why they speak of Christ as only a great cosmic teacher. For those who really understand the full significance of Christ, this is simply nonsense.

Humankind is coming of age through our modern spiritual science, through the concepts, ideas, and images that are linked with our life after death and thus with our entire soul life. For spiritual science can be understood by every person who wants to understand its findings. It strives to give people what each individual soul can truly achieve on its own, not by following the religious founders, as in earlier times. And although it must be individual researchers who make the results of this science of the spirit available today, they do so in a form that can be understood by everyone who wants to. I have often emphasized that it is a complete misunderstanding to say spiritual science must also be believed. When people say this, it is because they are so crammed full with materialistic prejudices that they do not look at what spiritual science really has to offer. As soon as it is examined, everything becomes understandable. One does not need clairvoyance for this; our ordinary understanding is enough to really grasp and comprehend all this gradually — of course, "gradually" will be inconvenient for some people.

In other words, spiritual science appeals to our understanding, making use of the opposite principle to the one used by the ancient religious founders. Their ideas gave something to human souls that awakened them spiritually and gave them strength to perceive in the etheric world, and that also means to lead a conscious life after death. Assimilating modern spiritual science will in turn give our soul the strength to develop the necessary power of thinking after death to consciously perceive its etheric environment. Both people of ancient times who followed their religious founders and modern people who are willing to understand spiritual science will be able to find their way after death.

Only *one* type of person will have difficulty in finding his or her way after death. In fact, this type will frequently not even experience a life after death, because it will have become so dulled and obscured. This sort of person is the dyed-in-the-wool materialist who clings to images of the physical world and does not want to develop any strength to perceive the world we enter after death. In terms of the soul-spiritual, to be a materialist really means the same as wanting to destroy one's eyes and ears in the physical world, gradually deadening one's senses. It is no different from someone saying, "These eyes — they can't be trusted, they provide only impressions of light. Away with them! These ears — they perceive only vibrations, not the one single truth. Get rid of them! Get rid of the senses, one by one!" To be a materialist in regard to the spiritual world makes as much sense as this attitude in regard to the sensory world. It is basically the same, as will be quite easy to see when we consider the reasoning presented by spiritual science.

Today I have attempted to explain from this perspective what it means to be in the spiritual world. I want to go on to explain a type of dream we will all recognize, because everyone has probably experienced a dream of this kind. I am speaking about dreams where we stand face to face with ourselves, so to speak. As I described earlier, usually the dream fabric unrolls itself before us, so to speak, and we have no clear awareness of ourselves at the time. It is only afterward that we reflect on the dream with self-consciousness.

There are also other dreams where we face ourselves objectively. And beyond simply seeing ourselves, as sometimes happens, we can also have the dream students often have, of sitting in school, trying to work out an arithmetic problem, but unable to solve the equation. Another person comes and easily finds the solution. The student really dreams that this happens. Well, you will understand that it was he himself who came and solved the problem. Thus, it is also possible that we face ourselves in this way without, however, recognizing ourselves. But that is not the important thing. In such a situation the I divides in two, as it were. It would be nice, wouldn't it, if in the physical world as well, the other ego appeared and immediately produced the right answer when we do not know something. Well, it does happen in dreams.

When we are dreaming, we are actually outside our physical and etheric bodies and only in the astral body and ego. While the type of dream described earlier gives us a glimpse of the etheric body, the ones where we face ourselves result from the astral body we took along revealing a part of itself to us and facing us with it. We perceive a portion of ourselves outside the physical body.

We do not perceive the astral body in ordinary life, but we can quite easily see part of it in sleep. It contains things we are not at all aware of when we are awake. I spoke earlier about the nature of the etheric body; it contains everything we have experienced. But now I have to tell you something quite strange—the astral body contains even those things we have not experienced. You see, our astral body is a rather complicated structure. It is in a certain sense built into us out of the spiritual world, and it contains not merely those things we already have in us now but also those we will learn in the future! They are already present there as a disposition. This astral body is much cleverer than we are. Therefore, when it reveals something of itself in our dreams, it can confront us with our self in a form that is much cleverer than we have become through physical life. If you bear this in mind—I say this now only as an aside and not as part of the lecture—it will throw some light on the "cleverness" of animals. They also have an astral body. It can bring out things that do not emerge in the ordinary lives of the animals. Many surprising things can reveal themselves there. For example, the astral body contains, believe it or not, all of mathematics, not only as far as we know it today, but also everything that still remains to be discovered. Nevertheless, if we wanted to read the mathematics contained there and read it consciously, we would have to do so actively by acquiring the necessary faculties.

Thus, it is a revelation of part of our astral body when we come face to face with ourselves in a dream. And many of the things that come to us as inner inspiration spring from these revelations of the astral body. In the same way hallucinations can occur under the circumstances I described earlier. The part of us that is cleverer than we usually are can, through a special disposition in our constitution, take on a voice of its own. Then we can be inspired, which would not happen if we used only our ordinary judgment in our physical body. But it is dangerous to give ourselves over to such things, because we cannot control them until we are able to penetrate them with our judgment. And since we cannot control them, Lucifer has easy access to all these developments, and we cannot keep him from directing them according to his intentions, rather than in accordance with the aims of the proper world order.

When we develop our inner forces, we learn to lead an inner life that makes us clairvoyant in the astral body. But you will see from what I have said that becoming clairvoyant in the astral body requires that we are always aware of facing ourselves, our own being. Just as we do not lead a healthy physical life if we are not fully conscious, so we do not lead a healthy soul life in the supersensible world if we do not see ourselves at all times. In the physical world we are ourselves; in the higher, spiritual world we have the same relationship to ourselves as we have here to a thought representing a past event. We inwardly look at such a thought and treat it as a memory. As we deal with a thought in this world, so we know in the spirit realm that we are looking at and observing ourselves. Our self must always be present when we experience things in the spiritual world. Basically, this is the only principle applying also to those things over which we have no control. In fact, in the realm of the spirit this principle allows us to master things, to become the controlling power. Our own being is the center of everything. Our own being shows us how we act in the spiritual world, revealing to us who we really are in the spiritual world.

If we are in the spiritual world and perceive something is incorrect, that means we are using the esoteric script incorrectly. Well, if we use the esoteric script incorrectly but perceive ourselves as the center of everything going on, we experience in our own being: You look like *this* because you did something wrong; now you have to put it right! We can see how we have acted by what we have become. We can compare this to how you would feel here in the physical world if you were not inside but outside yourself. For example, if you said to someone, "It is now half past eleven" — something that is not true — and look at yourself, you see how you stick your tongue out at yourself. You say, "This isn't you!" And then you start to correct yourself and say what is true, "It is now twenty past nine." At that moment your tongue goes back in. Similarly, you can tell whether you are acting correctly in the spiritual world by looking at yourself.

Such grotesque images may serve to characterize these things, which should be taken much more seriously than everything said about the physical world. The point is to gain an understanding of the supersensible realm through the power of thinking we already possess in the physical world. That way we free our thinking, which otherwise remains bound to our physical environment.

In earlier times people had a basic, atavistic clairvoyance. It was possible for them to have Imaginations, even Inspirations. But in contrast to this earlier stage, we have now reached an advanced stage and can form ideas about the physical world. When people still possessed an atavistic clairvoyance, they could not think properly. For proper thinking to develop, the strength used earlier in clairvoyance had to be applied to thinking. Some people nowadays develop clairvoyant faculties at certain times in their life by methods other than those described by spiritual science. This is because they have inherited these faculties from earlier times and they have not yet achieved sound judgment in those areas of life where they are clairvoyant. But we are approaching the time when sound judgment must be present before clairvoyance can be developed on the basis of such mature and balanced judgment.

In other words, when people these days show certain psychic abilities, a certain clairvoyance, without having done serious exercises, without having studied spiritual science — which, if applied in the right way, can be the best exercise to bring out the old clairvoyance — this does not mean that they are more advanced than everyone else, but rather that they are lagging behind. Having atavistic abilities today does not mean one has reached the stage of clear thinking. The more advanced soul is clearly the one that comes to sound judgments out of its ordinary understanding — and this ordinary understanding is completely sufficient to grasp spiritual science if one is free of preconceived notions.

We are making a great mistake if we allow atavistic clairvoyant abilities to impress us. We are on the wrong track if we believe such a person's soul is particularly advanced. That this soul shows such abilities means that it has failed to go through certain things that had to be experienced in the age of clairvoyance. Therefore, that soul is now catching up on what was missed earlier. It is quite grotesque when people involved in spiritual science believe that someone who displays a certain clairvoyance without having studied spiritual science must have been someone important in a previous life. Such a person was quite certainly less important than someone displaying sound judgment about things.

Now it is very important that our movement should try to build a certain circle of people who see through these things, who truly and thoroughly understand them and can reach the following insight: We need spiritual science in our time because only by understanding it can we progress.

This is very important. There are, of course, childhood illnesses in all areas of life, and naturally also in spiritual streams entering the world. And one can understand easily enough why spiritual science has childhood illnesses because it tries to give human beings the results that were achieved by clairvoyant consciousness. But you can see how we have to describe this. We have to say that becoming clairvoyant in the way humanity needs it now and in the future does not appeal to people's love of comfort and convenience. It requires a great deal more than just waiting for things to happen. Participation at every moment, self-control and the capacity for self-observation are required to reach the spiritual world. This must be widely understood. It is much easier to wait for clairvoyance to approach us like a dream, streaming to and fro. People want to experience the spirit realm in the same way they experience the world of the senses. This is a remnant from past periods of our history. In ancient clairvoyance, things were experienced in such a way that people did not really "know" them. This is probably why even today people want to experience the spirit realm in such a way that they do not actually "know" it. We do not properly appreciate what we know for sure. When we do arithmetic, for example, we follow certain set methods, without being much involved in what we are doing. When we add up five and seven, we are not really participating in the sense referred to here; we are not fully present in what we *do*. That is why people do not like it if others have developed their own view of the world. As soon as you can show people something you have come to know without this inner participation, they are happy, exceedingly happy! But when someone demonstrates knowledge of the spiritual world and knows of it in such a way that he is involved, then people say, "Oh, he knows it! That is a completely conscious process and not objective." But if someone comes along and has had a vision whose origin he cannot explain, people say, "That is objective, completely objective! We can believe this person."

The most important aspect of our spiritual science is to develop clear ideas. Spiritual science is still relatively new; therefore, now that people's longing for the spiritual world and knowledge of it has awakened, they want to connect with everything still coming up from the old world of clairvoyance. They gather all these old things and believe they are doing something quite special in preserving them.

However, our task is to see clearly in this field! It must be clear to us that there is nothing inferior about giving advice in full consciousness on a matter of spiritual healing. But most people will appreciate indications given by someone "above" the situation, who yields himself to quite obscure feelings and does not "know" things, much more because his statements result in the dark, blissful feeling: This is the result of something unknown! Everywhere we hear people saying that things they can grasp are of no interest to them. They have come for the inexplicable —*that* is supreme, divine!

Believe me, the individual truths of spiritual science must gradually enter our souls, and at the same time we must have a clear and sure sense for the conditions I have just touched upon. I have spoken about these conditions to show, beginning with the nature of dreams, that true clairvoyance requires the kind of active work by the soul we can compare with writing. I wrote *The Threshold of the Spiritual World* with the aim of clarifying these matters more and more. Those who understand my book will grasp the vital nerve, the keynote of our movement. I have to emphasize again and again—in spite of having said it frequently over the years — because so much depends on this: Those who really want to gain access to spiritual science have to acquire a healthy sense for the things that truly belong to it. Then we will gradually develop into a Society that can set itself the task of having a genuinely healing effect on everything belonging to cultural life.

Next time, we will continue to talk about what we began today as a description of the world of dreams based on the spiritual world.

LECTURE TWO

UNDERSTANDING THE SPIRITUAL WORLD

PART TWO

Berlin, May 12, 1914

Out of his conviction that we live in and are always surrounded by the spiritual world, the German philosopher Johann Gottlieb Fichte said:[1] "I do not need to wait until I am removed from the things around me in the physical world to gain entry into the spirit realm. I already exist and live in the latter much more truly than in the former. It is my only firm basis, and the eternal life I took possession of long ago is the sole reason why I still wish to continue the earthly one. Heaven does not lie beyond the grave; it is here already, pervading all of nature and its light rises in every pure heart."[2]

It is good to draw attention to such a statement, for in our time many people would have us believe that only stupid, superstitious characters or at least those inclined to fantasy speak of the spiritual world and have views on it. Interestingly enough, even those people who want to make us believe it is silly to talk of the spiritual world constantly speak of Fichte and others like him. So it is good if at least some people know that those with an anthroposophical outlook are of one mind with all the people who have carried throughout history a true knowledge and understanding of the spiritual world in their hearts, or at least a striving —in the highest and most noble sense of the word — for these things. And when materialists mention Fichte and pull this or that passage from his writings as it suits them, it is good when anthroposophically inclined souls know where Fichte's confidence in life, his courage for living, and his belief in life come from — they have their origin in his loyal adherence to the conviction that the human soul lives in the spiritual world and has a spiritual existence. When you hear a man such as Fichte quoted — as you know, he wrote the *Addresses to the German Nation* in difficult times — you should always be aware in your hearts that he had the strength to say what he said because he knew: The best part of me always lives in the spiritual world even while I am living in my physical body.[3] The spiritual world surrounds me everywhere. This is true for others too; Fichte is only an example. People like Fichte were aware that their words were filled with a strength gained through a knowledge of the spiritual world that supported and worked on their souls.

There is another reason why it is good to recall such facts from time to time. After Fichte had delivered his lectures *The Way Toward the Blessed Life,* which can be said to contain his life's teachings, to a small group of people, his audience asked him to have the lectures printed. The lectures had made a great impression on them, and they asked him to publish them because more people ought to have access to Fichte's encouragement for living, to his beautiful and noble striving for knowledge. And Fichte, strong, forceful, fired with the highest enthusiasm for his cause, made the following interesting remark in the foreword to these lectures:

> I was, I might almost say, persuaded to publish these lectures by friends among the audience who had a favorable opinion of them. And because of the way I work, the most certain way never to complete them would have been to revise them once more for publication. Let it be my friends' responsibility, then, if they are not received as anticipated. I for my part have become so confused by

> the public at large when I see the endless bewilderment that greets every powerful idea, and also the thanks accorded to everyone who endeavors to do right, that I am unable to make a decision in matters of this kind and no longer know either how to speak to this public or whether it is even worth the effort to address it by means of the printing presses.[4]

I want to quote this remark particularly because it shows how very alone Fichte felt then — 108 years ago now —with his tidings of the spiritual world in view of the general attitudes and spirit of the times. And yet, we cannot help but feel that anthroposophy is the fulfillment of what the great minds in human history longed and strove for in their endeavors. In view of the apathy and lack of judgment shown spiritual science today, we must evoke in our souls the harmony we can achieve with these great minds through our spiritual science to encourage and strengthen us. Nevertheless, it may take a long time even for those who are sympathetic with spiritual science to find the right inner energy to develop a feeling for the impulse it should give our culture. I mention this again only because I would like to see your hearts filled not only with the right kind of ideas about the spiritual world itself but also with the right kind of attitudes and feelings about our relationship to the spirit realm and our entire environment.

It is easy to see why spiritual science meets with incomprehension and misunderstanding in trying to establish itself in the world at large. Just try to understand how an ordinary citizen, a product of modern thinking, who has not really come into contact with anything spiritual, might relate to spiritual science. He has heard claims of one kind or another about the spiritual world. What must he do? Well, people have no choice but to try and make sense of these ideas on the basis of their own concepts. However, the ordinary person of our time does not possess any concepts that could help him grasp what true spiritual science says about the realm of the spirit. To begin with, he lacks the thoughts, concepts, and ideas to do this. He tries to penetrate what he is told with his ideas, which, of course, originated on quite a different level. How, then, is he supposed to avoid misunderstanding? How can we expect him to understand?

The central point in our relationship to spiritual science is to acquire new concepts, new ideas that we did not have before we encountered spiritual science and that we cannot bring with us from the outside, but have to learn gradually. This realization is fundamental for a right attitude of soul toward this spiritual stream. Consider the basic fact, namely, that spiritual science is to enable us to understand the spiritual world outside us. In the course of this year, we have heard many descriptions and all kinds of information about the spiritual world. We have always tried to enlarge our concepts and ideas so that we can really grasp properly what is going on in the realm of the spirit. For example, we speak about beings of the higher hierarchies, and you know what we say about them. We also speak of the souls of the dead as they exist between death and a new birth, and you know what we say about them. However, we must never forget that in speaking about these things we cannot use the concepts we learn in today's world or we will run into misunderstandings. Therefore I want to draw your attention to a concept you have already learned about, but I would like us to consider it in detail by examining how essential it has been to our various talks.

The physical world makes its impressions on our senses, and we try to understand this world with ideas and concepts tied to our nervous system, to our brain. When we look at this process, we find the central element is that we perceive the world. By looking at things, we perceive the human realm, human beings as physical beings, the animal, plant, and mineral kingdoms, clouds, mountains, rivers, oceans, stars, sun, and moon. We perceive these things to the extent that they are physical entities. We look at them, see their colors, hear their sounds, feel their warmth — in short, we perceive them. This is a perfectly correct description of our relationship to the physical world. But as soon as we look at the world of the spirit, we should feel the need for another expression than "I perceive," because it is not quite correct to say "I perceive the beings of the spiritual world." We need to understand that all so-called perception of the spiritual world is quite different from that on the physical plane. As we grow into the realm of the spirit and approach it, we have the impression that we are perceived. Here on earth we are, in a certain sense, the highest physical beings. A stone, a plant, or an animal might say they are perceived by human beings. And in terms of our physical body, we can say we are perceived by beings of our own kind. We are also perceived from the moment we grow into the spiritual world. The spiritual beings look down at us, and in a certain sense we become objects to them. It is indeed a first sign of having entered the spiritual world when we are perceived.

As I said in my last lecture, the way to rise toward the spiritual beings is to grow up to the level of their capabilities so that our being is perceived by them.[5] That is how it is with regard to the higher hierarchies. We learn to see ourselves grow into a state of mind allowing us to feel we are perceived by the higher beings of the hierarchy of angels. Then as we develop further, we are perceived by those of the hierarchy of archangels, and so on. This feeling that we are looked at, that the will of spiritual beings is affecting us, is what I mean when I say "We are perceived." We have to be quite clear about this and must not think that growing into the spiritual world is just a continuation of the panorama surrounding us in the physical world. Our whole soul mood changes because we become aware that we are living in the spiritual world, and that what we experience there is the feeling that the beings of the higher hierarchies perceive us. Their forces flow into us and are at work in us when we do something, when we act.

These things can best be explained with specific descriptions. So without any presumption — let me stress it again: without any presumption — and in all modesty, let me present the following example to show you what our relationship to the spiritual world is really like. When we undertake some work here on earth — whether it is spiritually inspired or not — we need forces coming to us from the physical realm. And these forces are outside our ordinary consciousness, of course. We cannot give them to ourselves; they are not really within our control. If you don't believe this, you can go to Dornach, to our building, and watch our friends there transforming large blocks of wood into capitals for the pillars and using their physical strength for this. Then you will have to admit that such forces come purely from the physical world. For my part, I admit quite openly that sometimes I wish I had more of this physical strength so I could help more with the work there. So, just as the strength of our hand muscles and other physical forces are involved in what we do physically, spiritual forces can also enter into our actions, flow into our souls from the spiritual world, and act from above downward, so to speak.

One of our tasks in past years was to express in our mystery plays what streams through our spiritual world view.[6] Spiritually perceived facts had to be projected onto a physical stage; to use the common expression, they had to be "staged." Such a production required new things compared with conventional stage productions. Over the years we have had to put on such plays with ever greater strength, one might say. But what I mean now refers not so much to external things, to what happens when everything is already there, but to the spiritual aspect of the matter.

In the early days of our work in spiritual science, a certain individual visited us.[7] This person not only developed a profound and warm-hearted interest in our teachings as we had to present them then at the start of our work, but was also imbued with a wonderful artistic spirit, which was fused completely with her personality. One could say in the true sense of the word that she was an objectively kind person. She quickly assimilated everything we could say about the content of spiritual science at that time. Then, and this was in the early years of our work here, she left the physical world. In the years that followed, she worked in the subconscious depths that our souls reach after death and tried to integrate what she had learned about our spiritual science with her artistic sensibility. A spirit body was being built up in which these two forces were at work: the fruitful views of spiritual science and her kind, energetic and understanding artistic spirit. Many years passed, and then recently, when we were working in Munich, whenever I had to make decisions about inner matters of the Munich performances, I was always aware that this individual was looking down on everything that is happening. It is, of course, not true that such a being would tell us how to do things. We must have our own abilities for that. But through the blessing flowing to us from such an individual, we can feel strengthened for the task at hand. We can feel her radiant spiritual eye and her warm, sincere interest flowing into the things we have to do.

Things like this can show us that after death the soul gradually changes into a being involved and active here on the physical plane. Once we are conscious of this, we feel the presence of such beings as guardian spirits supporting us in the tasks we have to do here in connection with the spiritual world. Then we can set about our tasks knowing that there is a being in the spiritual world who protects our work.

Now you can see the concrete insight that should permeate our life in regard to the spiritual world. We gradually come to know that the dead do not really die, but merely move to another place. They still participate in what we do. This insight will be more than a vague feeling for us; we will gradually learn to point to the areas where they are active. We will learn to feel them with us when we need forces we cannot find on the physical plane, when we need support from higher regions. For the souls who have passed through death possess forces different from those on the physical plane, because they take the material for their development at that stage from another world. We can feel the true inner deepening we can gain by taking up spiritual science, not just in the form of abstract theories, but in lively understanding of concrete particulars. We can then realize the blessing our theories of spiritual science and also the whole spiritual stream connected with it bestow upon all human life.

Of course, I assume such explanations in a group like this are taken with the necessary reverence, for that is the only way we can proceed from the abstract to the concrete.

Let us look at the example of another person who left the physical world a short time ago. This man had been associated with us for five years and had gradually united the best of his being with the knowledge resulting from spiritual science.[8] For many years, he was physically ill and had to fight against the attacks from his sick body. He truly demonstrated the triumph of mind over matter, particularly considering the strength he needed to create his last poems. From samples you have heard you already know the wonderfully poetic, intimate characterization of the spiritual world this man achieved. People will get many valuable insights when his last volume of poems appears in a few weeks.[9] The author of this volume cannot witness its publication; yet it will show us how wonderfully his spiritual life triumphed over the physical body. When I spoke about his poetry in Leipzig late last year, I used an expression in a way similar to a person, or even a child, saying "the rose is red."[10] Such a statement can be quite correct without anyone needing to "know" the rose is red. In the same way, I knew then in Leipzig that I could use the expression I chose and that it was correct. Out of an inner necessity, I said his poetry not only reveals a wonderful expression of our world view, but one could almost say these poems have an aura! Something had entered this man's soul and taken hold of his personality so that words not only flowed from him but also contained something akin to an aura. In a nutshell, that is what I said and what I felt to be true. It is only now that I know why I said this. Of course, we can only know after death what the individual who wrote these poems intended to do in the spiritual world, what he was preparing for. He suffered much because his physical organism was deteriorating. But while his body was deteriorating, something developed in the soul far beyond the physical body, something that turned out to be quite different from what he initially thought it was. This new quality lived in the depths of his soul, and its light became ever brighter the closer his physical body came to destruction. And now we can see something shining in the spiritual world that prepared itself here on earth.

Let me use a picture to explain what I mean. Nature is everywhere around us in all its beauty and glory. Surely, anyone sensitive to the beauty of nature will think I was justified when I said here some time ago that a person may visit all the art galleries of Italy, finally go up to the Swiss mountains to see a sunrise, and then have the feeling that the spiritual beings who paint the sunrise are greater painters still than those who paint on canvas.[11] Even though this is true, we must also admit that while we may admire the beauty of nature with complete abandon, we find it infinitely precious when we see how a painting by Raphael, Leonardo da Vinci, or another artist, presents the content of the artist's soul as well as nature's beauty.[12] In art, we see a physical expression of what the soul can give us, enriching what we take from nature. I want to use this analogy to prepare your heart to understand what I want to say next.

The individual I have just mentioned is now in the spiritual world, and the spiritual formations once trapped in his body are now free of it. Here on earth we have his wonderful poetry, but in the spiritual world we find lighting up what grew out of the Imaginations that were prepared here during his long illness, and that now form the basis of his spirit body. A splendid cosmic image! In these Imaginations lives a wonderful element from the cosmos that is to the direct perceptions of spiritual research what a wonderful painting is to a direct experience of the beauty of nature. When the spirit realm presents itself to the inner gaze in the Imaginations of a human soul, and we ourselves perceive it also, infinitely much will be revealed to us. In fact, it is almost as though the cosmos is perceived twice; once as it appears directly to our clairvoyant gaze, and then again as it is revealed to the clairvoyant gaze through what a human soul attained on earth through much suffering and vigorous striving for spiritual knowledge. I do not have to remind you that all these things must be understood as karma; no soul can acquire anything of this sort merely by force of will. Whether such things are granted us lies in the grace of the wise cosmic powers. During the time we spend on earth, we, and others as well, must take care to remain on earth as long as possible and in as healthy a condition as possible. This should go without saying, but these things are so easily misunderstood. No one should ever attempt to do anything to cause suffering. That must not happen, and, in any case, nothing could be achieved this way. Therefore, no worse and more false conclusion can be drawn from all this than to decide to make oneself suffer in some way just to achieve something.

With these specific examples I wanted to present two ideas. The first is that spiritual beings send their powers to us through the gaze of their spiritual eyes, as I tried to show with the example of the guardian soul of our artistic work. The other idea demonstrates the inner wisdom of the cosmic powers, which allows us to see in the spiritual world what an individuality has drawn from his earthly existence. This can then in turn enrich our perception of the spiritual world, just as artistic perception enriches our experience of the physical world.

I could say much more now about individualities who are blessed to carry what they absorbed from the anthroposophical world view into the spiritual world. However, the time for that has not yet come. I quoted these two cases because I believe such concrete and familiar examples can help us better understand the thoughts and ideas necessary for real access to the spiritual world. We must adhere to those concepts from the beginning, if we really do want such access. After all, we meet in smaller groups so that we can, in a sense, speak the language we have gradually developed for the description of spiritual life. Through spiritual science, we can progress to where we no longer talk in general terms about the spirit around us, just as we do not talk of nature around us in general terms, either. We speak not only of nature this and nature that, but of grass in the meadows, corn in a field, trees on a hillside, clouds, and so on. Gradually we have to learn to speak of the spiritual world in equally specific terms. Therefore, I like to talk of the spiritual world in concrete terms by discussing a guardian soul such as the one I mentioned today in connection with our artistic work, or by mentioning a soul whose form after death mirrors the forces emanating from the spiritual cosmos itself, forces this soul gathered while the body was overtaken by infirmity here on earth. This soul teaches us things we would not easily learn otherwise.

People like this friend, whom you knew, become the best helpers to aid spiritual science in fulfilling its task in the world. Since spiritual science is received in many quarters with misunderstanding, contempt, and hostility, we may feel that it will truly be very difficult to make any progress toward achieving its real purpose. However, the insights we discussed today evoke the encouraging thought that those who have passed through the gate of death become true witnesses for the true nature and purpose of spiritual science. I would like this thought to speak to our hearts and souls.

With this in mind, we cannot help believing that even if it takes longer than our lifetime, spiritual science will become part of the spiritual progress of humanity. This thought can give us courage to face what confronts us in certain quarters; it can give us courage in our conviction that more and more people will come to see the need to develop new concepts, new ideas, sentiments, and attitudes for a true understanding of the spiritual world.

I hope explanations like these also provide a proper context for our role in our spiritual movement. Let us accept examples such as those with reverence, and let us also draw from them what is relevant for our convictions so that we will be strong enough to bear the brunt of attacks from the outside. People outside our movement approach us only with the concepts they have learned in the world, and we should not be terribly surprised that they impose those concepts on what they find out about us. There are major problems in the relationship between spiritual science and the outer world's statements and judgments about it.

As you know—and as one of our dear members told you last time out of firsthand experience and an enthusiastic heart — we want to begin a real, true work of art in Dornach, near Basel; a work of art that is a result of our world view. Everything depends on there being a few people in the world who really understand what we intend to do. It is crucial that we do not let only those people judge this endeavor who want to describe it in terms derived from the outside world. No matter how good people's intentions are, if they approach our building with conventional concepts, they will only get a conventional description.

For instance, we can see now that newspapers in every language are saying things about the building in Dornach that can easily sweep away in a short time what we have struggled for many years to achieve — by not telling the public what it does not understand anyway. The newspapers have asked, What age are we living in? Is this still the age of materialism? An enormous temple is being built — and so on. And they have described the columns in this temple as supposedly linked by pentagrams and such. Seeing this, we can only wonder where such descriptions of the things that should develop out of our spiritual stream will lead. Such descriptions are now circulating through the media—it's terrible!

We do not need to go into detail, but the most painful thing is that the original article, which was the basis for all the others, was the work of a good-natured soul who wanted to understand us and do a great service to the movement by writing about it. We even showed him around to avoid the worst excesses of reporting. We showed him, for example, that there is really no pentagram to be seen, but that in one place the seeker's mind has to feel its way cautiously and subtly to a perception of a pentagram. Then we found that although we had asked this person not to write anything that smacks in any way of journalism, he could not do anything else, and did not use the concepts and ideas learned from us but instead only those that can be picked up on the streets of our modern culture! It is deeply painful to me to see how our original intentions and aims are now presented in the newspapers. The articles and clichés are passed on from one paper to the next and are translated into every language, and in each language another distortion and more stupidity are added. Of course, it is not hard to understand what happens when the aims of our serious and sincere spiritual science clash with what the outer world can understand. But I want to show you how solemnly and reverently we must approach our cause. It is important that we be aware how deep our understanding for the tasks of spiritual science in the world must be.

You may want to ask why we could not continue to work with our concepts modestly and anonymously even among those who cannot understand us, as we did *before* we started the building in Dornach. Well, people in the present age have their eyes focused on the physical level. Spiritual things go unnoticed, but that a building is being erected in Dornach cannot be ignored. Such questions are, of course, completely unproductive and also irrelevant. What matters is that we should have a proper appreciation for and understanding of our cause in our hearts. I do not say this to accuse or criticize anyone, but to remind you once again how earnestly we must try to understand the new that is to grow in us to counterbalance what comes from the world outside, particularly in the opinions of other people. What comes from outside is not part of what our souls really need and thirst for. They need spiritual science and yearn for it. Therefore, we must put the temptations and seduction of materialistic thinking, particularly that due to spiritual arrogance, in proper perspective. We must not be blinded when we encounter such views and attitudes everywhere in the external world, but must find the strength within ourselves to participate fully in this world and to seek in ourselves the impulse for a proper relationship to the world around us. Then spiritual science can really become something that warms and strengthens us inwardly. It can give us foundations for our judgment so that we are not blinded by external influences, which may approach us with authority and power and therefore can deceive us again and again about the ability of our age to understand spiritual science.

This is what I wanted to present again to your souls today. For now as summer approaches and our meetings will become less frequent, we want to be certain of one thing: The impulses of spiritual science should live in our souls independently of time and space. They should be alive in us regardless of whether we meet more often or less often. What is important is the character of our meetings, that we really bring them to life in us. That is what I wanted to discuss with you today.

LECTURE THREE

AWAKENING SPIRITUAL THOUGHTS

Basel, May 5, 1914

I am very glad that we can meet here today and take a break, so to speak, for a while from the work on our new building in Dornach.[1] But I thought it would be impossible to gather here so near our building without also discussing anthroposophical matters. I hope we can do this more often in the course of the year; otherwise our friends working on the building will not have as many opportunities to attend such meetings as they do when they are not working on our building.

Let us start with some thoughts on the life of the spirit that might be useful in considering what meaning spiritual science and living with anthroposophy can have for us, for our soul. People new to anthroposophical thinking, feeling, and perception may think we should not worry about the life of the spirit, about the spiritual world, since we enter the spiritual world anyway after death (even a materialist might say this) and will there learn all we need to know about it. Why should we not be satisfied in this life between birth and death simply to do what is necessary for life in the physical world; why is it wrong when we just fulfill our duties in the physical world, and leave matters concerning the spiritual world in the realm of the uncertain and indefinite? One could hear these words often during the time when the tide of materialism engulfed human development, especially in the last third of the nineteenth century. And it was by no means the most morally reprehensible souls who said: While on earth, let us concentrate on our tasks here and leave the rest for the world we enter after death.

Now, let us talk about something that can be grasped immediately by anyone who begins to concern himself with — I do not even want to say spiritual science — but with truly logical thinking. We actually spend only part of our time between birth and death in the physical world, namely, our waking time. And even people who have not yet thought much about the spiritual world, but who can think logically, would have to admit that with our conscious mind we know as little about life in sleep as we do about life after death. And certainly no one can deny that we continue to live in sleep — unless such a person were prepared to accept that we really die every evening and are created anew each morning. That is unlikely, but the truly logical person will be equally unable to accept that the whole human being is really present in a sleeping body lying in bed.

The fact that we sleep regularly should at least make people think. And then they will be motivated to reflect on what spiritual science has to offer. In particular, the natural sciences will more and more realize that our soul is not present in our physical body when we sleep. In fact, they will reach this conclusion on their own before the end of this century of scientific development. Then they will look to spiritual science for answers to their questions. They will be forced by their own conclusions to realize that our soul-spiritual being is really not connected with our physical body when we are sleeping. It will then become ever more important for people in the twentieth century to know something about sleep. Therefore let us begin today and get an idea of what people in our century will have to know about the nature of sleep.

We know from our studies in spiritual science that when we fall asleep, two members of our being, the ego and the astral body, leave the physical and etheric bodies. Where are the ego and the astral body when we are asleep? To begin with, we can say they are in the spiritual world. Of course, we are always in the spirit realm, because the latter is not separated from the physical world, but surrounds us just as air envelops us everywhere. We are always in the spiritual world, even when we are awake.

However, we inhabit it in a different way when we are asleep than when we are awake. Now, it may be sufficient for the immediate needs of spiritual science to describe this situation by saying that in sleep our ego and astral body are outside our physical and etheric bodies. But then we would actually be telling only half the truth. It is the same as saying the sun sets here at night; because the sun in fact sets then only for us in Europe. We know this does not apply to all the inhabitants of the earth. Fundamentally, the ego and astral body leave our physical and etheric bodies properly, we might say, completely, only after death. In sleep they actually leave only the blood and nervous system. But when the "sun" of our being, namely, the ego and astral body, sets in relation to our blood and nervous system, which they penetrate during the day, it rises for the other half of our being, that is, for the other organs.

Our ego and astral body do just what the sun does, which shines here during the day and when it sets for us, it rises for the people on the other side of the earth. When ego and astral body "set" for our blood and nervous system, they rise for the other organs and are linked all the more strongly with them.

These other organs, to which our ego and astral body are connected when we sleep, have been constructed out of the spirit, as has everything else in the world. And the remarkable fact is that while we are sleeping, we strongly influence these other organs of our body with our ego and astral body. During the day, our ego and astral body work strongly upon our blood and nervous system, but they influence our other organs, all those not part of the blood and nervous system but which affect the blood from the nerves, when we are asleep.

From this follows that it is of some consequence how we enter sleep with our ego and astral body. Materialists will not care much about what happens in sleep to their ego and astral body, which they never mention anyway. However, those who understand these things will know that the organs that are not part of the blood and nervous system and do not manifest in our conscious existence are dependent on those aspects of our ego and astral body that are active in sleep.

Let me illustrate this with an obvious example. As we know, people today are haunted by a fear we can compare with the medieval fear of ghosts. It is the fear of germs. Objectively, both states of fear are the same. Both fit their respective age: People of the Middle Ages held a certain belief in the spiritual world; therefore quite naturally they had a fear of spiritual beings. The modern age has lost this belief in the spiritual world; it believes in material things. It therefore has a fear of material beings, be they ever so small. Objectively speaking, the greatest difference we might find between the two periods is that ghosts are at any rate sizable and respectable. The tiny germs, on the other hand, are nothing much to write home about as far as frightening people is concerned. Now of course I do not mean to imply by this that we should encourage germs, and that it is good to have as many as possible. That is certainly not the implication. Still, germs certainly exist and ghosts existed also, especially as far as those people who held a real belief in the spiritual world are concerned. Thus, they do not even differ in terms of reality.

However, the important point we want to make today is that germs can become dangerous only if they are allowed to flourish. Germs should not be allowed to flourish. Even materialists will agree with this statement, but they will no longer agree with us if we proceed further and, from the standpoint of proper spiritual science, speak about the most favorable conditions for germs. Germs flourish most intensively when we take nothing but materialistic thoughts into sleep with us. There is no better way to encourage them to flourish than to enter sleep with only materialistic ideas, and then to work from the spiritual world with the ego and the astral body on those organs that are not part of the blood and the nervous system. The only other method that is just as good is to live in the center of an epidemic or endemic illness and to think of nothing but the sickness all around, filled only with a fear of getting sick. That would be equally effective. If fear of the illness is the only thing created in such a place and one goes to sleep at night with that thought, it produces afterimages, Imaginations impregnated with fear. That is a good method of cultivating and nurturing germs. If this fear can be reduced even a little by, for example, active love and, while tending the sick, forgetting for a time that one might also be infected, the conditions are less favorable for the germs.

These issues are not raised in anthroposophy merely to play on human egotism, but to describe the facts of the spiritual world. This concrete case demonstrates that in real life we cannot avoid dealing with the spiritual world, because it is the basis for our actions between going to sleep and waking up. If people were given thoughts that lead them away from materialism and spur them on to active love out of the spirit, it would serve the future of humanity better. Then infinitely more productive work could be achieved than through all the preparations now being developed by materialistic science against germs. In the course of this century, the insight has to spread more and more widely that the spiritual world is by no means irrelevant to our physical life, but is of essential importance to it because we are in the spiritual world between going to sleep and waking up, and continue to affect the physical body from there. Even if this is not immediately obvious, it is nevertheless true.

Now, we will have to get used to the fact that the direct healing powers of spiritual science have to work through the human community if we are to see these matters in the right light. What does it mean that some individual here or there enters the spiritual world in sleep with thoughts turned toward the realm of the spirit, while all around other people nourish and nurture the germ world with their materialistic thoughts, materialistic feelings, and with fears, which are always connected with materialism? What is the real nature of germs? Well, here we come to a subject essential for human life. When we see the air around us filled with different species of birds and the water filled with fishes, when we observe the life forms that creep along the earth and others frolicking on it and revealing themselves to our senses, we are looking at beings we can correctly describe as creatures of the developing Godhead in one form or another, even if they are occasionally harmful. But in the case of germ-like creatures resident and active in other living beings, in plants, animals, or humans, we are dealing with creations of Ahriman. To understand the existence of such creatures correctly we must know that they express spiritual facts, namely the relationship between human beings and Ahriman. This relationship is established through a materialistic attitude and purely egotistical states of fear. We see the conditions allowing the existence of such parasitic beings correctly if we realize that they are a symptom of Ahriman intervening in the world.

Clearly, then, it is not a matter of indifference whether we take materialistic or spiritual ideas with us into the spiritual world when we fall asleep. As soon as we realize this, we can no longer claim it is irrelevant whether or not we know of the spirit in this world. We have to start at a specific point if we really want to understand the great importance of spiritual scientific research for our life between birth and death.

It will become increasingly clear to us how this earthly life is connected with spiritual life. We rely on nature, which is on a lower level than we are, for our nourishment. For some time after death, the dead derive their nourishment from the ideas and the unconscious emotions that we here on earth take into sleep with us. Those who have died perceive a tremendous difference between people who in their waking life are filled only with materialistic feelings and ideas and also take them into sleep, and others who are wholly filled with spiritual ideas while awake and who continue to be filled with them in sleep. The two types of people are as different in their effect on the dead as a barren region where no food can grow, where people would starve, and a fruitful area that offers nourishment in abundance. For many years after death, the dead draw a vitality from the souls sleeping here on earth filled with spiritual content, a vitality that is similar, only transposed into the spiritual realm, to what we draw in our physical life from the beings of the kingdoms of nature below us. We literally turn ourselves into fruitful pastures for the dead when we fill ourselves with the ideas of spiritual science. And we turn ourselves into barren ground and starve the dead if we take only materialistic ideas and attitudes into sleep.

It is not out of the enthusiasm that leads to the establishment of many other associations and societies that we speak of spiritual science in these times. Rather, the urge to speak about it comes out of necessity and the heartfelt realization that in the twentieth century people will need it. Regardless of outer circumstances, those who fully understand how much the world needs spiritual science cannot help but talk about its results and share it with their fellow human beings.

The power of the words at our disposal seems much too weak to meet the necessity of making spiritual science ever more available to those who would otherwise sink deeper and deeper into materialism.

Let us think about the nature of our relationship to the dead we were connected with in life, whom we can clearly visualize, and of whom we often think. What is our relationship to those who have died, apart from offering them spiritual nourishment by taking spiritual thoughts into sleep? What is our relationship with the dead in waking life?

If the dead draw nourishment from the content of our souls in sleep, then every thought that enters the spiritual world and is concerned with it and its beings can be perceived by the dead. On the other hand, if we do not cultivate such thoughts, the dead are deprived of them. Ideas related only to the material world, to things in nature, live in our souls in such a way that the dead cannot perceive them. These ideas, however scholarly or wise, are meaningless for the dead. As soon as we have thoughts about the spiritual world, not only the living but also the dead have immediate access to them. That is why we have often recommended that our friends read silently to an individual with whom they were closely connected and who has passed on to the spiritual world. One forms an image of the person and then, while thinking about him or her, one reads on a subject related to the spiritual world. The dead can then participate in the process, which is important. Although the dead are in the world we know through spiritual science, thoughts about the spiritual world must be produced on earth. The dead must perceive more than the spiritual world around them; they need the thoughts of those who live on earth, thoughts that for them are like perceptions.

The most important and the most beautiful thing we can give the dead is to read to them in the way I have just described. We can give something to the dead by reading on a spiritual subject. And if you doubt that this is useful, since the deceased is in the spiritual world anyway, just think that we can be surrounded by things and beings in the physical world, yet may not understand them. The understanding has to be acquired. Thus, although the deceased is in the spiritual world, thoughts from earth have to flow to him. Illuminating thoughts must flow up to those regions where the dead dwell, just as rain streams down from the clouds as a blessing to the physical world.

All these examples show that it is infinitely important even for the physical world to experience the spiritual world in thought. Obviously, we cannot wait until after death for knowledge about the spiritual world. In truth, a thorough study of the spiritual world shows us that we are not on earth for nothing; we are here to learn something that can be learned only on earth — a possession of such value that the living can give it even to the dead.

The close connection between our earth existence and life immediately after death also manifests in many other respects, but it is difficult to talk about this connection in concrete terms, because the words can so easily be misunderstood. People are greatly inclined to prejudice, and whenever a subject, such as the spiritual world and its beings, is discussed, certain motives of the heart provoke misunderstandings. When I tell of an individual case where there is this or that connection between a person's life here on earth and after death, people all too easily jump to the wrong conclusions out of a very understandable self-centeredness and apply the description of a particular case to themselves. They are tempted to think that things are quite different in their case; therefore, they will not experience something this beautiful after death. Instead of deriving satisfaction from the events described, the listeners out of egotism feel that their experience will not be equally exceptional after death.

As soon as we do more than just speak in general terms and deal with specific cases, we must develop selflessness so we can observe someone else's destiny without drawing conclusions about our own life. Then we will not worry that if the same does not happen to us, we are missing out on what is being described. These and similar reactions provide grounds for misunderstandings, which I want to avoid.

A short time ago, a very dear friend of ours died, and many of us attended his cremation.[2] He would have celebrated his forty-third birthday tomorrow, on May 6. In the final years of his life, he suffered much. I would like to tell here, parenthetically as it were, a wonderful story from his last years as his wife told it to me.[3] During his great suffering, our friend fought not against admitting to himself that he had to suffer, but against saying that he was ill. He was not ill, he said. He suffered, yes, but he was not ill, and he was adamant that such a statement should not be taken as quibbling but as something meaningful. This definition, "I suffer, but I am not ill," arose from his awareness that what he carried within him as spiritual science, what supported and carried him inwardly, defeated all attacks of illness. He was aware that he suffered, but the health of his soul is so great that, when he compared it to his physical condition, he could not call himself ill. This definition is very important and well-suited to permeate our soul as a feeling.

Anyway, we saw how the person concerned spent his last years on earth in a sick body, in a suffering body. Yet he did not see himself as sick but only as suffering. If we compare that with the spiritual life that has now begun for our friend, we will have a worthy image of what connects our earth existence with life after death. It is a fact of the spiritual world that a series of Imaginations was prepared in his body, a body that showed the symptoms of illness.

A series of Imaginations, powerful Imaginations, lived, so to speak, in the sick limbs. He was completely filled with the content of the spiritual worlds. They lived in him in such a way that they worked on all those organs we are usually not as aware of as we are of our brain and nervous system, that is, organs we experience on a more subconscious level. These powerful Imaginations lived in these organs, and all the more so, the more outwardly ill these organs became. They prepared themselves and now face the soul of the deceased as a mighty tableau of the spiritual world. Now he is living in the images that were trapped in his sick organs, especially in his final years. They prepared themselves in such intensity that they now surround him as his spiritual world.

It is impossible to see more beautiful worlds, or to see the spiritual cosmos more perfectly and more beautifully, than those that blossom and unfold in spiritual art, which cannot be observed better anywhere else than through such a situation. Here, on the physical plane, an artist can create in beauty a piece of the world, so that the image on canvas or in marble lets us see more of the world than we do on our own. All of this, however, pales into insignificance in comparison to the spiritual world seen as it is and also as it arises and blossoms forth from the soul of the deceased who has been prepared by his karma in the way I have described. How he was prepared will be clear from his poetic works, which are now being printed and will appear soon.[4] His poetry reveals that this kind of spiritual life and passage into the spiritual world after death are intimately connected with what we have for many years called the Christ-Impulse. The Christ-Impulse, in the sense spiritual science speaks of it, is beautifully alive in our friend's poetry.

In this connection I want to add something that can truly lead us to feel the relationship between the world of our earthly life and the one we pass through between death and a new birth. I will not present this connection with abstract thoughts, but so you can grasp it at the level of feeling. You see, one can be either stupid or clever here on the physical plane; one can even be a scholar — in the life after death it is of little importance whether one was stupid, clever, or learned if all these qualities relate only to the things of the physical world. Our thoughts about the material world may be ever so clever; they will be of no use to us once we have passed through death. They will then no longer have any meaning. After death we need thoughts, ideas, and feelings that do not relate to the physical world, because only those have meaning then.

Now, I would like to put this in a somewhat grotesque, paradoxical way. Do not be put off by the paradox; what I want to say will become clear immediately. Let us assume that someone refuses to have any thoughts that are not called forth by sensory perception. As soon as anything impinges on him and thoughts begin to develop, he says: I do not want you. I proceed only on the basis of what my eyes see and my ears hear. That is what I want to think about. Stop bothering me with anything else; I will not bother with it . . . . Such a person does not accumulate any strength that can be used after death. He is blind when entering the world between death and new birth.

Let us assume now that someone else has a lively imagination, but cannot be bothered to approach spiritual science and learn things slowly and gradually. He finds it much easier to develop ideas about the spiritual world from his imagination, to fantasize about the spiritual world. This person has ideas concerning the sense world as well as all kinds of fantasies about the realm of the spirit. Such an individual would not enter the spiritual world as a blind person, but will have soul forces that will enable him to see in the spiritual world. However, such people will be as we are when our vision in the physical world is impaired and we see things inaccurately as a result. Such inaccurate vision is a lot worse in the spiritual world than on the physical plane because there it leads to confusion at every turn. What I have just said, even if it seems grotesque at first, shows us that we need ideas reaching beyond the life of the senses if we really want to become citizens of the spiritual world, as we must. And unless we get our bearings from beyond the sense world, we will live in the spiritual world in a crippled state, as do those who take in only ideas related to the sensory realm and those who allow their imagination to run wild.

Various founders of religions appeared throughout history to prevent people from having thoughts triggered purely by physical objects or by fantasies about the spiritual world. If we look at these personalities and the teachings they gave humanity, we find that the aim of all these religious founders was to offer people ideas about the supersensible world that would allow them to enter it healthy and whole, not crippled. The founders of our religions provided ideas that met the needs of their particular time and culture.

Our age is different from the past and requires us to grow up into mature human beings. Please do not take this in a superficial, merely external sense, but in a deeply inward one. We have to reach maturity and find the path into the spiritual world through our souls. The ancient founders of our religions spoke to a humanity that was not yet mature. They addressed people at a stage through which all our souls have also passed. These ancient religious leaders knew their times, and also knew that they could not speak in the same way to a humanity moving further toward the future. For humanity must develop toward maturity and independence.

If people of ancient times had either restricted themselves to sense impressions or had reached for the products of their imagination, in both cases they would have entered the spiritual world crippled or at the very least in a confused state. At that point a leader appeared, bringing true ideas from the spiritual world. People then said that they themselves did not gain access to the spiritual world through sensory perception or use of the imagination, but rather through Zarathustra, Buddha, or Krishna, who stimulated thoughts in them that allowed them to enter the realm of the spirit.[5] In our time human beings must come of age, regardless of whether the ego causes confusion or blindness. The Mystery of Golgotha took place so that we can find the way into the spiritual world as independent beings. Religious leaders no longer appear in history as they did in earlier times.

Those who compare Christ to the ancient religious teachers do not understand anything about him. In the first place, Christ worked through a deed, the ancient religious leaders through their teachings. To describe him merely as a teacher of humanity means not knowing at all who Christ is. The essential thing about him is the deed he performed, which began as a consequence of his baptism by John and ended with the crucifixion on Golgotha. What was done there for humanity is spiritually all-important. What happened there is what can permeate human souls ever since then, namely, the experience St. Paul described as "Not I, but Christ in me." Indeed, Christ has become the path into the spiritual world because he brought it into this world. He brought us the spiritual world we need if we are not to be crippled or blind after death.

It is quite possible these days to deny Christ and claim that there is no evidence that Christ lived in the physical world in the body of Jesus of Nazareth. In fact, people have even produced evidence showing there was no historical Christ. But with that they merely prove that they missed the point. If Christ had chiseled into a rock for all future generations, "I was here," then those future generations would have known he existed from the sensory world, and they would not have needed to believe it. His deep significance, the possibility of redemption, is precisely that this was not the case, that we cannot comprehend him through our senses but have to accept him with the forces of the spirit. Seen in this light, we find Christ intimately connected with those things that even here on earth lift human beings beyond the sense-perceptible world into the spiritual realm. None of this exists for those who cannot raise themselves to the spiritual world, because they cannot escape their doubts.

In this context it can be a great relief for someone fully involved in modern culture, in science and art, to come across a view of Christ that is appropriate to our modern civilization, namely the anthroposophical view of Christ presented in spiritual science. Much can be learnt from it, for example, how to view the physical world correctly. Oh, the physical world — where is it headed these days? I hinted at some of these things recently in a public lecture, but now I can be more explicit.[6] Of course, we have to admire materialist civilization and all the achievements of technology, industry, and so on. An immense amount of intellectual energy has flowed into these things; they have taken up a great deal of human energy. But who benefits from these intellectual efforts? Insofar as they satisfy the material needs of modern humanity, they serve Ahriman. Christ Jesus experienced the temptation by Ahriman. Ordinary human souls could certainly not survive the sudden shock of such an experience. For us the temptation has to be diluted. But as a consequence of this dilution of temptation, Ahriman can say to us: Yes, think only with the power of your science, with all those things you can discover through science applied to technology, industry, and so on. Use only those things for your thinking and apply them to nothing but physical experience; that suits me fine. It fits in well with my aims, says Ahriman, if you are unable to see me.

You might well despise reason and knowledge, the supreme achievements of human beings; thus you are absolutely mine — at least as long as you do not see me. I will instill the drive in you to use reason and knowledge only for earthly things!

Something else is required to counterbalance the service we render Ahriman. It is therefore important that we gather everything modern technology and so on can accomplish to build something with it that is not to serve our outer existence, but only our spiritual life.

In ancient times, people presented sacrifices to the gods, the first fruits of the field and of the herd. I do not intend to talk about the meaning of sacrifice today, but you can see what it could signify presented in a form appropriate to modern times. When the first fruits had been sacrificed to the gods, the people partook of the remainder. Spiritual science is certainly not based on false asceticism. It will not be guilty of the absurdity of ranting and raving against modern culture with all its material blessings. On the contrary, it recognizes their value. But if it wants to avoid serving only Ahriman, it has to sacrifice something of the first fruits of this external material culture to the gods.

So you see, there is a profound thinking underlying the building that is growing outside on the hill at Dornach: We want to offer the first fruits of modern civilization to the gods. Everything is different now from the way it was in the times our souls passed through in previous incarnations. And we have to understand the nature of our current task just as we understood what we had to do in our earlier incarnations when we were guided by spiritual luminaries. That is especially difficult now because we have to take into account not only the nature of our time but also our soul qualities. In addition, we can no longer rely on the external authority that supported the founders of religions; we have to work with quite different forces. Christ was the Word;

in the same way true spiritual science wishes to work only through the word and must not use any other means.

Such reflections give us an insight into the connection between the spiritual world and our world here on earth. And no matter where we begin, we see the Mystery of Golgotha radiating toward us as the heart and soul of such reflections. But we must not forget that we have to become mature, truly mature, so that we can understand what spiritual science is meant to be. We must never forget that it must exist because humanity must come of age.

It is completely true that humanity descended from higher spiritual regions and has moved away from the old atavistic clairvoyance by developing a world view based on reason and systematic thinking. We have to take this progress in evolution seriously. We must realize we live at a time when it is our mission to develop our thinking, to advance through our thinking, and to learn through studying. Spiritual science is our basis, our point of departure. We must try to immerse ourselves in these ideas so that they stimulate within us what our souls need in the future. What spiritual science offers can be understood by everyone. Those who claim one cannot understand the contents of spiritual science, but must believe it, speak without knowing how these things really are.

We must not be misled when we meet people who have not advanced by means of intellectual understanding, but have certain psychic abilities that seem to appear spontaneously. Based on our understanding of the mission of spiritual science, we know that souls can now think only because the clairvoyance of an earlier age has been suppressed. People with natural clairvoyance, which was not acquired through inner effort, must be seen as persons who have remained at an earlier evolutionary stage and who should therefore receive special care in our Society, rather than be considered particularly advanced. It would be an incorrect judgment if we were to consider such souls particularly mature, as having experienced particularly high incarnations. People with a natural gift of clairvoyance have gone through far less than those who are thinkers nowadays. These things have to be properly understood in our Society. Then it would be possible (and it is my duty to say this) for our Society to be a place where such souls with psychic powers can find care and be guided on the right path. Our Society could give them what they cannot get anywhere else: order in their soul. But to make that possible most of the members of our Society must have a profound inner knowledge of the mission of true spiritual science in the present. If that happened, then the case that so saddened us in recent days could not recur. I am referring to a member, who joined in the belief our Society would care for clairvoyant psychic forces, but then found here a captive audience and took on the role of a prophet. Such an event opens the door to all those things that, if they were to prevail, would turn our Society into the exact opposite of what it should be according to the intentions of the spiritual forces supporting it.

Unfortunately, we have had to suffer the case of. . . ., who came from a country in the north. He might have become a good member if he had worked quietly on developing his psychic powers. Instead, he was immediately surrounded by a kind of aura. He presented himself everywhere as a healer in a way we can only consider regrettable. It became necessary to announce that he could no longer be considered a member of our Society. For it would be turned into the exact opposite of what it should be if we failed to carefully draw attention to psychic phenomena that are not imbued with true spiritual power, which, after all, is the true power of Christ. Christ, not psychic powers, must work in us. These circumstances must be handled so as to make it clear that our Society will have nothing to do with this.

It knows no other sanction than the one used in the last few days. Unfortunately, a step had to be taken we otherwise oppose in principle: a member had to be expelled.

This cannot be separated from a serious and worthy concept of the mission of the Anthroposophical Society. And certainly you will understand that it is only with great sorrow one lives through the events that had to be lived through here in the last few days. We are in principle opposed to all expulsions and yet could not avoid expelling someone in such a case. It will happen less and less frequently if our dear friends continue to take to heart the things that have been said so often and that were also the subject of tonight's talk. With that I will conclude my remarks, my dear friends, and entrust them to your souls.

LECTURE FOUR

THE PRESENCE OF THE DEAD IN OUR LIFE

Paris, May 25, 1914

First of all, my dear friends, I want to say that I am very glad we are meeting here at this branch of the Anthroposophical Society today. I remember with great pleasure our meeting last year, and my greeting at the beginning of this lecture is as sincere and heartfelt as that memory.[1]

Today I want to talk about a subject closely connected with the core of our anthroposophical movement. All the results of our spiritual movement are based on research that may be called clairvoyant. While I have often emphasized that our heart, mind, and feelings are primarily affected by anthroposophical truths, we cannot ignore that these truths depend on clairvoyant research, which is an expression of a soul condition different from that of everyday life. It appears to lead us away from the things that seem so important to us in daily life, but in reality, clairvoyant research leads us right into the heart of truly human life.

Today, I do not want to speak about the paths to clairvoyant research since I have already described them in *Knowledge of the Higher Worlds and Its Attainment*.[2] Rather, I would like to characterize the condition and mood of soul that develops as a consequence of this research.

Indeed we must bear in mind that if we follow the paths to clairvoyant research, we will feel completely different from our usual self. What happens to our soul when it becomes clairvoyant can be compared with our dreams, which are like surrogate clairvoyance. When we dream, we live in a world of images, which contains nothing of what we call "the sensation of touching an object outside us." In our dreams there is usually nothing we can compare with normal ego consciousness. If any aspect of our ego does appear in our dreams, it seems to be separate from us, almost like another being outside us. We face our ego like a separate entity. Thus, we can speak of a doubling of the ego. However, in dreams we perceive only the part of ourselves that has separated, not the subjective ego. All statements apparently contradicting what I have just said can be traced to the fact that most people know of their dreams only from memory, and cannot remember that in the actual dream the subjective ego was extinguished.

The images of clairvoyant research resemble dreams because in both the sense of touch and the subjective ego are absent. A clairvoyant recalling his or her experiences must feel that the clairvoyant reality is permeable and, unlike physical objects, offers no resistance to touch. In the physical world we have ego awareness because we know: I am here, the object is outside me. However, in clairvoyant perception we are inside the object, not separated from what we perceive. Consequently, the individual objects are not fixed and distinct as physical ones, but are in continuous movement and transformation. Objects in the physical world are fixed because we can touch them and because they offer us boundaries, which objects of clairvoyant perception do not have. The same thing that causes our ego to fuse with the objects of clairvoyant perception also forces us to be very careful when we encounter what we call in the physical world another ego, another human being.

Let us first look at what happens when we encounter a person who has died through our clairvoyant faculties. Such an encounter can come about when the figure of the deceased approaches us in clairvoyant perception like a very vivid dream image, looking every bit as we remember the person looked in life. However, this is not the usual type of such encounters, but a rare exception.

Another possibility is that we clairvoyantly perceive a dead person who has taken on the form of either a living or another dead individual, and thus does not appear in his own form. The appearance of the deceased, then, is of very little relevance in identifying him. Perhaps we were particularly fond of another dead person or have a particularly close friendship with a living one; the deceased approaching us can then take on the form of either of those other individuals. In other words, we lack all the usual means of identifying the ego and appearance of a person in the physical world. It will help us find our way to remember that the appearance or form is not at all important; a being is meeting us in one form or another, and we need to note what this being does. If we take our time and carefully observe the image before us, we will realize that, based on everything we know about the individual in question, this person could not act the way he does in the clairvoyant sphere; his actions are totally out of character. We will often encounter a contradiction between the person appearing to us and his actions.

If we allow our feelings to accompany these actions, ignoring the individual's appearance, we will get a sense in the depths of our soul telling us what being we are actually dealing with. Let me repeat that we are guided by a feeling that rises up from the depths of our soul, for that is very important. The individual's appearance in the clairvoyant sphere seems to resemble a physical figure but can be as different from the being really present as the signs for the word "house" are from the actual house. Since we can read, we do not concentrate on the signs that make up the word "house" and do not describe the shape of the letters, but instead we get right to the concept "house." In the same way, we learn in true clairvoyance to move from the figure we perceive to the actual being. That is why we speak of reading the occult script, in the true sense of the word. That is, we move inwardly and actively from the vision to the reality it expresses just as written words express a reality.

How can we develop this ability to go beyond the appearance, the immediate vision? We do so, above all, by looking at new ideas and concepts we will need if we want to understand the clairvoyant sphere — new, that is, in contrast to the ideas we use in the physical world.

In the physical world we look at an object or a being and say, quite rightly, I perceive that being, that object. We perceive the plant, mineral, and animal kingdoms, the realm of physical human beings, as well as clouds, mountains, rivers, stars, sun, and moon. The feeling expressed in the words "I perceive" undergoes a transformation when we enter the clairvoyant sphere.

Let me try to explain this with an analogy, though it may sound simplistic. If you were a plant, how would you relate to people perceiving you? If this plant had consciousness and could speak, it would have to say: People look at me, I am perceived by them. Of course, we say: I perceive the plant, but at its level of consciousness, the plant would have to say that it was perceived by human beings. It is this feeling of being perceived, being looked at, we must acquire in relation to the beings of the clairvoyant sphere. For example, concerning the beings of the first hierarchy, the angels, we must be aware that strictly speaking it is not correct to say "I perceive an angel," but we have to say "I feel an angel perceiving me."

Based on our Copernican world view, we know full well that the sun does not move. Nevertheless, we say that it rises and moves across the sky, thus contradicting our better knowledge. Similarly, in everyday language we can say that we see an angel. But that is not the truth. We would actually have to say that we feel ourselves seen or perceived by an angel. If we said we experience the being of an angel or of a dead person and can feel it, we would speak the truth from the clairvoyant point of view.

Perhaps an example from clairvoyant observation will help you understand this. More than ten years ago, at the beginning of our work with spiritual science, a dear friend of ours worked with us for a short time.[3] This individual possessed not only enthusiasm for what we could give her in the early stages of spiritual science, but also a profound artistic sensitivity and understanding. One could not help but love this person, a love that may well be described as objective because of her qualities. Having worked with us for a relatively short time and having learned a great deal about the results of spiritual science, she left the physical world. There is no need to go into the next four or five years after her death, so let me get directly to what happened after that. In 1909, we presented our mystery plays in Munich, preceded, to our great delight, by *Children of Lucifer* by our highly respected friend Edouard Schuré.[4] Whatever you may think about the way the plays were produced then and later, we had to present them the way we did. The circumstances under which we had to work on the performances were such that we needed an impulse from the spiritual world, an impulse that also included the artistic aspect we wanted to incorporate. Now, I can assure you that even at that time, in 1909, and even more so in later years, I always felt a specific spiritual impulse as I was working on the arrangements for the performances.

You see, when we have work to do in the physical world, we need not only intellect and skills but also the strength of our muscles. Our muscles objectively help us; they are given to us, unlike the intellectual capacities we ourselves dwell in. Now, in dealing with matters of the spirit we need forces from the spiritual world to combine with our own, just as we need the strength of our muscles for physical action. In the case I mentioned, the impulse from the individual who had left the physical world in 1904 entered more and more into our artistic work on the Munich plays. To describe what happened, I would have to say the impulses from this individual came down from the spirit plane and flowed into my intentions, into my work. She was the patron of our work.

We develop the right feelings toward the dead if we become aware that their spiritual gaze — if I may use that expression — and their powers focus on us; they look at us, act in us, and add to our strength.

To experience such a spiritual fact in the right way, we need to develop a very specific type of selflessness and a capacity for love. That is why I stressed that one could love that person objectively, as it were, because of her qualities; one had to love her because she was as she was. A subjective love, a love arising out of personal needs, can easily be egotistical and can potentially keep us from finding the right relationship to such a dead individual. The difference between the right love, the selfless love we have for such a person, and selfish love becomes perfectly obvious in clairvoyant experience.

Let us assume such a person would want to help us after her death, but we cannot develop true selfless love for her. Her spiritual gaze, her spiritual will streaming toward us would then be like a burning sensation, causing a piercing, burning feeling in our soul. If we can feel and maintain a selfless love, this stream, her spiritual gaze as it were, flows into our soul like a feeling of warm mildness and pours itself into our thoughts, imagination, feeling, and willing. It is out of this feeling that we recognize who the dead person is and not on the basis of his or her appearance, because the dead may manifest in the guise of a person we feel close to at the moment. The form in which the beings of the higher world appear to us—and after death we are all beings of a higher, spiritual world — depends on our subjective nature, on what we habitually see, think, and feel. The reality is what we feel for the being manifest before us, how we receive what comes to us from this being. Regardless of what Joan of Arc said about the appearance of the higher beings in her visions, the occultist who is able to investigate these things knows that it was always the genius of the French nation who stood behind them.[5]

I described how we can feel the gaze of spiritual beings resting upon us and their will flowing into our souls. To learn this is analogous to learning to read on the physical plane. Those who merely want to describe their visions would be like people describing the shape of the letters on a page rather than their meaning. This shows you how easy it is to have preconceived notions about the experiences in the spiritual realm. Naturally, it seems most obvious to attach great importance to the description of what the vision looked like. However, what really matters is what lies behind the veil of perception and is expressed in the images of the vision.

Thus, in the course of occult development, the soul immerses itself in specific moods and inner states different from those of our everyday life. We have entered the world of the hierarchy of angels and the hierarchy, or we could also say hierarchies, of the dead as soon as our occult exercises have brought us to the stage where the sense of touch characteristic of the physical world no longer exists, and where a person's appearance is no longer characteristic of the I concerned. Then our thinking changes, and we no longer have thoughts in the sense we have them here in the physical world. In that world, every thought takes on the form of an elemental being. In the physical world, our thoughts can agree or contradict each other. In this other world we enter, thoughts encounter other thoughts as real beings, either loving or hating each other. We begin to feel our way into a world of many thought beings. And in those living thought beings, we really feel what we usually call "life." Here life and thinking are united, whereas they are completely separate in the physical world.

When we speak on the physical plane and tell our thoughts to someone, we have the feeling that our thoughts come from our soul, that we have to remember them at this particular moment. Speaking as a true occultist and not someone who just tells his experiences from memory, we will feel that our thoughts arise as living beings. We must be glad if we are blessed at the right moment with the approach of a thought as a real being.

When you express your thoughts in the physical world, for example, as a lecturer, you will find it easier to give a talk for the thirtieth time than you did the first time. If, however, you speak as an occultist, thoughts always have to approach you and then depart again. Just as someone paying you the thirtieth visit had to make his way to you thirty times, the *living* thought we express for the thirtieth time has to come to us thirty times as it did the first time; our memory is of absolutely no use here.

If you express an idea on the physical level and someone is sitting in a corner thinking, "I don't like that nonsense, I hate it," you will not be particularly bothered by it. You have prepared your ideas and present them regardless of the positive or negative thoughts of someone in the audience. But if as an esotericist you let thoughts approach you, they could be delayed and kept away by someone who hates them or who hates the speaker. And the forces blocking that thought must be overcome because we are dealing with living beings and not merely with abstract ideas.

These two examples show that as soon as we enter the sphere of clairvoyance, we are immersed in living and weaving thoughts. It is as if these thoughts are no longer subjective and as if you yourself are no longer within yourself, as if you are living outside in the wide world.

When you are in this world of living and weaving thoughts, you are in the hierarchy of angels. And just as our physical world is everywhere filled with air, the world of the hierarchy of angels is filled with the mild warmth I spoke about earlier that the beings of this hierarchy pour out. When our inner development has brought us to the stage where we can live in this spiritual atmosphere of streaming mildness, we feel the spiritual eyes of the hierarchy of angels resting on our souls.

Now, in our earthly life, we have certain ideals and think about them abstractly. As we think of them, we feel obligated to pursue these ideals. In the clairvoyant sphere, however, there are no abstract ideals. There ideals are living beings of the hierarchy of angels and flow through spiritual space, looking at us with warmth.

In the physical world, we may have ideals, know them well, and yet we may not do anything to apply them. Our emotions, and perhaps passions, can tempt us to shirk them. However, if we knowingly ignore an ideal in the clairvoyant sphere, we feel the spiritual gaze of a being of the hierarchy of angels directed at us with reproach, and this reproach burns. In the spiritual world, ignoring an ideal is thus a reality, and a being of the hierarchy of angels reproaches us. Their gaze makes us feel the reproach; it is the reproach we feel.

You see, learning to develop a real feeling for ideals is one way of entering the world of the hierarchy of angels. Limiting our consciousness to the physical plane may lead us to think that nothing will happen if we are too lazy to act on our ideals. However, we can learn to feel that if we do not act on an ideal, then, regardless of other consequences, the world becomes different from what it would have been had we followed our ideal. We are on the way to the hierarchy of angels when we begin to see that not acting on our ideals is something real, and when we can transform this insight into a genuine feeling. Transforming and vitalizing our feelings allows our souls to grow into the higher worlds.

Through continued esoteric training, we can rise to an even higher level, that of the hierarchy of archangels. If we ignore the angels, we feel reproach. With the archangels we feel reproach as well as a real effect on our being. The strength and power of the archangels works through our I when we live in their world.

For example, a few months ago we lost a very dear friend when he left the physical plane. A profound poet, he had quickly found his way into the anthroposophical world view in the last five years, and the feelings it evoked in him are beautifully reflected in his recent poetry.[6] From the time he joined us, and even before that, he had been struggling with an infirm and deteriorating body. The more his body deteriorated, the more his soul was filled with poetry that reflected our world view. Only a short time has elapsed since his death, and so one cannot yet say that this individual possesses a clearly existing consciousness. Nevertheless, the first stages of his development in the existence after death can be seen. The astral body, now separated from the physical and living in the spiritual world, reveals the most wonderful tableaux of cosmic development as we understand it in spiritual science. Having left the deteriorated physical body, the astral body has become so illuminated, comparatively speaking, that it can present the clairvoyant observer with a complete picture of cosmic evolution.

Let me use an analogy to explain what I mean. We can love nature and admire it, and still appreciate a beautiful painting that recreates what we have seen in nature. Similarly, we can be uplifted when what we have seen in the clairvoyant sphere lights up again, as a cosmic painting, so to speak, in an astral body of a person who has died. The astral body of our departed friend reveals after death what it absorbed, at first unconsciously but later also consciously, in the course of his anthroposophical development when the beings of the hierarchy of archangels worked actively on the poetical transformation of his anthroposophical thoughts and ideas.

Our progress in our esoteric development can be called mystical, because it is initially the inner progress of the soul. We transform our ordinary personality and gradually reach a new state. This step-by-step growth of the soul is mystical progress because at first it is experienced inwardly. As soon as we can perceive the mildness looking down from the spiritual world, we are objectively in the world of the angels, which reveals itself to us. And as soon as we can recognize that real forces of strength and power enter into us, we are in the realm of the archangels. With each stage of inner mystical progress we have to enter another world.

However, if we fail to develop selflessness and reach the stage of living in the world of the angels while remaining selfish and unloving, then we carry the self intended for the physical world into their realm. Instead of feeling the mild gaze and will of the angels upon us, we feel that other spiritual powers are able to ascend through us. Instead of gazing at us from outside, they have been released by us, shall we say, from their underworld while we were raised to a higher world. Instead of being overshadowed, or rather illuminated, by the world of the angels, we experience the luciferic beings that emerge from us.

Then, if we reach the stage of mystical development allowing us to enter the world of the archangels — without, however, having first developed the wish to receive by grace the influences of the spiritual world, we carry our self up into their realm. As a result, instead of being strengthened and imbued with the power of the archangels, the beings of the ahrimanic world emerge from us and surround us.

At first glance, the idea that the world of Lucifer appears in the realm of the angels and the world of Ahriman in that of the archangels seems terrible. However, there is really nothing awful about this. Lucifer and Ahriman are in any case higher beings than we are. Lucifer can be described as an archangel left behind at an earlier stage of evolution, Ahriman as a spirit of personality also left behind at an earlier stage. The terrible thing is not that we encounter Lucifer and Ahriman, but that we encounter them without recognizing them for who they are. Encountering Lucifer in the world of the angels really means encountering the spirit of beauty, the spirit of freedom. But the all-important thing is that we recognize Lucifer and his hosts as soon as we enter the world of the angels. The same is true of Ahriman in the realm of the archangels. Lucifer and Ahriman unleashed in the higher worlds is terrible only if we do not recognize them as we release them, because then they control us without our knowledge. It is important that we face them consciously.

When we have advanced in our mystical development to the level of living in the world of the angels and want to continue there with really fruitful occultism, we have to look for Lucifer as soon as we expect the spiritual gaze of the angels to rest on us. Lucifer must be present — and if we cannot find him, he is within us. But it is very important that Lucifer is outside us in this realm, so that we can face him.

These facts about Lucifer and Ahriman, angels and archangels, explain the nature of revelation in the higher worlds. From our viewpoint in the physical world, we are easily led to believe that Lucifer and Ahriman are evil powers. But when we enter the higher world, this no longer has any meaning. In the clairvoyant sphere, Lucifer and Ahriman have to be present just as much as the angels and archangels. However, we do not perceive them the same way. We identify the angels and archangels not by their appearance, but we know the angels by the mildness that flows from them into us, and recognize the archangels by allowing their strength and power to flow into our feeling and will. Lucifer and Ahriman appear to us as figures, merely transposed into the spiritual world; we cannot touch them, but we can approach them as spiritual projections of the physical world. Clearly, it is important that we learn in our mystical clairvoyant development to see forms in the higher world and to be aware that we are seen, that a higher will focuses on us.

You see, higher development does not consist merely in acquiring clairvoyant faculties, but in developing a certain state of soul, a certain attitude or relationship to the beings of the higher world. This new attitude and state of soul must be developed hand in hand with the training of our clairvoyant faculties. In other words, we must learn not only to see in the spiritual world but also to read in it. Reading is not meant here in the narrow sense of a simple learning process, but as something we acquire through transforming our feelings and sensations. It is important to keep in mind that a split of our personality occurs when clairvoyance begins, and we reach a revelation of the higher worlds. Our earthly personality is left behind, and a new one is acquired on ascending into a higher world. And just as the beings of the higher hierarchies look at us in the higher world, so we perceive our own ordinary personality from a higher perspective. Our higher self discards the lower one and observes it. So, to make valid statements about the higher worlds we had better wait until we are able to say: That is you; the person you see in your clairvoyant vision is yourself. "That is you" on the higher level corresponds to "this is I" on the physical one.

Now remember when you were eight or thirteen or fifteen years old and try to reconstruct from your memory a small part of your life at that time. Try to recall as vividly as possible your thinking in those years. Then concentrate on your current feelings about the girl or boy you were at eight, thirteen, or fifteen. As soon as we move from the physical level to the higher world, the present moment we live in now becomes a memory of the kind we have just recalled. We look back at our current existence on the physical level and at what we may still become during the remainder of our physical life in the same way you look back to your experiences at eight, thirteen, or fifteen from your vantage point in the present moment.

Everything we consider part of ourselves on the physical level, such as our feelings, thoughts, ideas, and actions, becomes a memory as soon as we enter the higher world. We look down at the physical world and become a memory to ourselves when we live in the higher world. We have to keep our experiences in the higher worlds separate from those in the physical realm, just as we distinguish between our present situation and an earlier one. Imagine a person who is forty years old and vividly remembers the feelings and abilities he or she had as an eight-year-old boy or girl. For instance, the person might be reading a book now, at the age of forty, and all of a sudden he or she begins to relate to the book as an eight-year-old would. That would be a confusion of the two attitudes, the two states of soul, and is analogous to what happens when we confuse our state of soul on the physical level with what is required in the higher worlds.

Of course, this has nothing to do with the fact that every unbiased person can understand what I say about the higher worlds; in other words, we do not merely have to believe these descriptions, but we can understand them if we approach them without preconceived ideas. People may object that we cannot describe the higher worlds with concepts, thoughts, and ideas from the physical world because the former are completely different from the latter. This objection makes as much sense as saying that we cannot give people an idea of what we mean by writing h-o-u-s-e; for them to understand that concept, we have to bring them a house.

We talk about physical facts and objects by means totally independent of the object or fact. So we can also describe phenomena of the spiritual world with what we understand on the physical plane. However, we cannot understand the higher worlds with our everyday concepts and ideas, but need to acquire others and expand our thinking. People who honestly tell us about the higher world must also extend our concepts beyond our everyday life; they must give us concepts that are new and different and yet comprehensible on the physical plane.

People find it difficult to understand genuine spiritual science and serious esotericism because they are so reluctant to expand their concepts. They want to understand the higher world and its revelations with the ideas they already have and don't want to create new ones. When people in our materialistic age hear lectures on the spiritual world, they believe all too easily that the esoteric world can be understood simply by looking at it. They think the shapes there may be slightly more delicate and more nebulous than in the physical world, but similar nevertheless. It may seem inconvenient to some that the serious occultist is expected to do more than merely follow instructions on how to see angels. A change in thinking is necessary, and the concept "angel" must include that we are perceived by them, that their spiritual gaze is focused on us.

Mystical development, or ascending to the higher worlds, cannot be separated from enriching and giving greater scope to our ideas, feelings, and soul impulses. To understand the higher worlds, we must not let our life of ideas remain as impoverished as it is on the physical plane.

To provide esoteric help for this enrichment, we are constructing our modest building in Dornach in a completely new style. That building is, of course, nowhere near the ideal, but it is a humble beginning. After all, we have only limited means at our disposal, despite the fact that our friends have done everything within their power for this project.

The spiritual impulses behind the building styles that developed in the third, the fourth, and in the current fifth post-Atlantean epoch included the task of guiding humanity to knowledge of the physical world. For example, Egyptian architecture initiated this development with its succinct geometrical forms. Greco-Roman architecture is like a marriage of soul and spirit with etheric and physical body. Here soul and spirit on the one hand and etheric body and physical body on the other connect in a state of complete equilibrium. The rising, pointed arches of the Gothic style are the first architectural attempt to rise again from the physical into the spiritual world.

If anthroposophy is to be represented in a building the next step must be to bring to life the living and weaving thought patterns themselves, flowing and pouring into space. Then we will see in physical form what Imagination and Inspiration reveal directly of the spiritual world. That is why the forms of the Dornach building are such that it is pointless to ask in materialist fashion what they symbolize and what their shapes stand for. They have to be taken on their own merit, since they are nothing more than immediate spiritual experiences poured out into spatial forms. We have attempted to transform everything that can be seen and experienced in the spirit into artistic form. So if people ask what a form stands for, they have misunderstood the building; for every form signifies only itself, just as our hands or head stand only for themselves and nothing else. Such a question also indicates a complete misunderstanding of our position in regard to occultism. We will be glad to leave behind the old theosophical nonsense of examining every fairy tale, every figure, and every myth for what it signifies and symbolizes.

All our forms really exist in the spiritual world and therefore express only themselves and nothing else. They are not symbols, but spiritual realities. You will not find a single pentagram throughout the building, no form of a pentagram, nothing to make you wonder what this or that form means. At most, there is one place where subtle forms could be interpreted as a pentagram, but so can every five-petaled flower. People may ask what our fourteen pillars mean, which are not shaped as pentagrams, but are five-sided for aesthetic reasons. They may wonder what the pillars supporting the cupolas mean besides representing spatial relations perceptible in the spiritual world. In reply we can only point out how materialistic our age is when even spiritual intentions must be clothed in materialist garments.

Our building will be understood if people stop asking what it symbolizes and instead think about what it is. They will understand our building when they realize it is better not to use any of the usual terms and the old verbal images to help our materialist age comprehend it. Spiritual science can at most be a synthesis of religions; unlike the ancient religions, it does not build temples, but rather a structure that expresses its innermost nature. This building can only be understood gradually, and only if we do not apply old words to this new development.

We know only too well that we can realize our intentions in Dornach only in the most modest, rudimentary way. But I ask only that you make a real effort to understand this humble beginning from the perspective and significance of our spiritual science. Try to understand what this simple beginning, paid for with considerable sacrifices, is aiming at. Any other attitude would be most disheartening.

Enough grand words and pompous phrases have been bandied about in the so-called occult movement. All we want is that even if our way of expressing things no longer exists fifty years from now, people will still say of our movement that it endeavored with every fiber to be totally sincere and honest. And the more modestly and simply, but thus perhaps the more objectively, we discuss what we wish to do, the better we serve our cause. Every word that is superfluous or returns to the old, convenient concepts does untold damage to what we are striving to achieve — please excuse me for saying this — honestly. If people understand us in this way, then perhaps the mood will arise that we need if we are really, in December at the earliest, to inaugurate our modest building without pomp and fuss.[7] The mood we need will be there only if we concentrate on our goals, even if we do not create a stir in our materialist age.

Please accept these words in the spirit of the serious intentions of our movement. They must fill our souls if this spiritual impulse is really to take root in our age. There is a real need for an honest spiritual movement that truly promotes the mystical life of the soul and allows revelations of the higher worlds to flow into this materialist age. Only when our friends understand this purpose and attitude of our spiritual movement, then and only then shall we be able to fulfill the task given us by the wise, guiding individualities in the spiritual world.

Based on what I have tried to explain today, I will speak to you the day after tomorrow about the progress in our understanding of Christ through the ages and about the position of our movement concerning the Christ.[8]

LECTURE FIVE

THE BLESSING OF THE DEAD

Paris, May 26, 1914

We have now reached a stage in human development where the study of spiritual matters must be based on the same foundations as the study of nature was three or four centuries ago.[1] Spiritual science intends to achieve similar things for knowledge of the spirit as Copernicus, Galileo, and Giordano Bruno did for the understanding of physical nature in their own time.[2] Of course, the systematic exploration of the spirit in our age encounters the same kind of resistance and hostility as the study and the concepts of the natural sciences did then. Spiritual science will be assimilated into our culture as slowly and with just as much difficulty as the natural sciences were.

We will investigate the spirit with processes of the human mind that are still unknown today, or at least unpopular with most people. Clairvoyant research, as we can call these processes, provides the foundation for spiritual science, and I am speaking to you today on that basis.

Clairvoyant research is discredited by the countless prejudices people have against it, and also by the widespread misuse of the term "clairvoyant investigation." That is why I want to say right now that I am not speaking from the standpoint of the occult knowledge so often promoted by charlatans these days, but based on the kind of clairvoyant, esoteric knowledge that can be supported even by people firmly grounded in serious research in the natural sciences who base their knowledge on genuine scientific facts. In terms of its inner logic, its mode of thinking, spiritual science belongs to the stream of modern thinking that includes the natural sciences. The two differ only in the areas they research. The natural sciences examine the world of nature, the physical phenomena around us, while spiritual science studies an area that must necessarily remain hidden to the natural sciences, namely, spiritual experience and spiritual beings. It is impossible to investigate spiritual facts and spiritual beings with the same abilities and methods that have allowed the natural sciences to celebrate ever greater triumphs in the course of the last few centuries. To investigate nature, we use only those mental powers and abilities we have because of the way we are put into this world, and because other people have taught them to us.

This combination of innate and acquired abilities is totally sufficient for the natural sciences, but it cannot provide knowledge of the spiritual world. For that we must use faculties that slumber, that are latent, to use a scientific term, in the depths of our soul during our everyday life.

We do not immediately apply the methods and procedures used to explore the outer world in our investigations as spiritual researchers. Rather, we work with them on the abilities and forces in the depths of our soul to make them effective in the spiritual world. These capabilities help us to understand the higher worlds only when they have been drawn out by ordinary human efforts.

For example, in everyday life and in conventional science, we learn about the external world through ideas we develop in our soul, but as researchers of the spirit, we first have to work with our thinking deep within us to develop abilities that are quite different from those we normally have. Spiritual science is basically in accord with the natural sciences, as we can see in its attempt to enter the spiritual world through spiritual chemistry. We cannot tell from the looks of it that water can be split into hydrogen and oxygen. Though water is liquid and does not burn, hydrogen is a combustible gas — clearly something quite different from water. We can use this as a metaphor for the spiritual process I am about to explain.

People are a combination of soul-spiritual and material-physical elements, just as water is a combination of hydrogen and oxygen. In "spiritual chemistry," we must separate the soul-spiritual from the material-physical elements just as water can be separated into hydrogen and oxygen. Clearly, just looking at people will tell us little about the nature of the soul-spiritual element.

The methods we use to separate the soul-spiritual from the material-physical in us—and this experiment of spiritual chemistry can be carried out only within us — are concentration and meditation. Meditation and concentration are not some kind of miraculous mental performance, but the highest level of mental processes whose lower, elementary levels we find also in our everyday life. Meditation is a devotion of the soul, raised to limitlessness, as we may experience in the most joyful religious feelings. Concentration is attentiveness, raised to limitlessness; we use it at a more basic level in ordinary life. By attentiveness in everyday life we mean not allowing our ideas and feelings to range freely over anything that catches our attention, but pulling ourselves together so that our soul focuses our interest on something specific, isolating it in our field of perception. There are no limits to how far this attentiveness can be increased, particularly by voluntarily focusing our soul on certain thoughts supplied by spiritual science. Ignoring everything else, all worries and upsets, sense impressions, will impulses, feeling, and thinking, we can center our inner forces completely on these thoughts for a certain amount of time. The content of what we are concentrating on is not as important as the inner activity and exercise of developing our attentiveness, our powers of concentration.

Focusing, concentrating the forces of the soul in this way is crucial. And regular training, often involving months, years, or even decades, depending on individual predisposition, is necessary for the soul to become strong enough to develop inner forces. Qualities otherwise merely slumbering in the soul are now called up by this boundless enhancement of attentiveness, by concentration. In the process we must develop the capacity in our soul to feel that through this inner activity the soul is increasingly able to tear itself away from the physical body. Indeed, this tearing away, this separation of the soul and spirit from the physical-material element, will happen more and more often as we continue the activities I have described. In the limited scope of a lecture, I can only briefly outline this principle of concentration, but you will find detailed descriptions of the individual exercises in my book *Knowledge of the Higher Worlds and Its Attainment*, translated into French as *L'Initiation*.[3]

Through practicing these methods we will learn to understand the meaning of the sentences, *I experience myself as a soul-spiritual being. I am active in myself without using my senses or my limbs. I have experiences independent of my body*. We have made progress when we can perceive our own body with all its physical attributes as separate and independent of our soul and spirit, just as we see a table or a chair in physical life. This is how we can begin to separate the soul's ability to think and form ideas from its physical tools, namely, the nervous system and the brain. Thus, we learn to live in thinking and the forming of ideas, fully aware that we are outside the nervous system and the brain, the physical instruments we normally use for these processes.

To put it more concretely, let me add that our first experience in this self-development is the realization that in thinking we live as though outside our head. We live in our weaving thoughts just as we do when we use our brain, but we know for sure that these thoughts are outside our head. The experience of immersing ourselves again in the brain and the nervous system after having been outside the head for some time remains indelibly with us. We feel the resistance of the substance of brain and nervous system such that the soul-spiritual that emerged from those physical organs needs to use force to reenter them. This is an unforgettable moment.

The method I have described also allows us to release the feeling and will activities of the soul, which is necessary for true spiritual research. To achieve this, we must raise devotion to the infinite. This enhanced devotion, which is also called meditation, is similar to what happens when we sleep. The sense organs are laid aside in sleep; there is no activity of the senses, and the limbs are at rest. While we sleep, we are given over to the general course of the world without contributing anything through our I, thinking, feeling, and willing to the course of events. We are unconscious in sleep; our consciousness dissolves into general darkness and obscurity. In meditation, we must voluntarily create the state sleep causes as natural necessity. The only difference is that sleep leads to a loss of consciousness, but intensified devotion leads to an enhanced awareness. As spiritual researchers, we must be able to silence our senses at will. We must divert them from all impressions of the external world and suppress the activity of our organs and limbs as we do in sleep. In terms of our body, we have to behave just as in sleep. However, in sleep we sink into unconsciousness, but in enhanced devotion controlled by our will we awaken into the divine-spiritual stream of cosmic forces. To this level of consciousness we then reach, our everyday consciousness is what sleep is to our ordinary state of consciousness.

If we persevere and patiently train our soul, we will be able to separate out, through a kind of spiritual chemistry, another soul capacity, namely, our thinking, so that it continues only in the soul-spiritual sphere. Similarly, through devotion we can gradually separate out that power of the soul we use in language, in speaking. As I am speaking to you now, I am using a soul-spiritual force that flows into my nerves and speech organs and uses them. Through the exercises described above, we can unfold this same power when the entire speech and nervous system are completely inactive. In this way, we discover in the depths of our soul a faculty we know nothing of in our everyday life, because it is employed in speech and the use of our speech organs. When we are not using this faculty, it lies dormant deep within our soul, but in spiritual research, it is drawn up and separated by spiritual chemistry, so to speak, from our physical speaking. If we learn to live in this weaving, hidden activity of language creation, we can recognize what we may call, perhaps inaccurately, the perception of the inner word, the spiritual word. As soon as we can control this hidden power, we can also detach our thinking and feeling from our personality, leave ourselves behind, and enter the spiritual world. Then we can perceive feeling and willing outside ourselves just as we did within us. We begin to know beings of will and feeling in the spiritual world, and we can perceive our own willing and feeling only when they are immersed in these beings.

Clairvoyant perception begins with the emancipation of the power of our thoughts from the physical body and continues with the freeing of our thinking and feeling. Clearly, then, we can know and truly experience encounters with other spiritual beings only by leaving our body and by immersing our own feeling and willing soul in the spiritual world. In view of the widespread opposition to spiritual science in our time, it is risky to give concrete examples; yet it is a risk I am willing to take. I am sure you will not mind that it is an example from my personal experience. After all, our own experiences are the examples we know best since they are the only ones where we are actually present for every detail.

Some time ago I had to solve a problem in my work.[4] I knew very well that the capacities I can develop in accordance with my constitution in this life would not suffice to perform the task, which was to understand the mentality of a certain historical period. I knew exactly what questions I had to answer, but I also realized that no matter how much I exerted my thinking, my thoughts were not strong enough to gain insight into this problem. It was like wanting to lift a weight but lacking the strength to do so. I tried to define the issue as clearly as possible and to develop the active will to find a solution one way or another. As far as I could, I tried to feel vividly the particular qualities of that period. I tried to get a vivid sense of its greatness, its color, and to project myself completely into that period. After I had repeated this inner soul activity often enough, I could feel a foreign willing and feeling enter my own. I was as sure of its presence as I am that the external object I see is not created by my looking at it, but exists independent of me and makes an impression on me.

From a materialistic point of view, people can easily object that this was nothing but an illusion, a deception, and that I did not know I was drawing out of my own soul what I thought were external influences. To avoid falling prey to illusion, hallucination, and fantasies in this field, we need true self-knowledge. Then we will begin to know what we can and cannot do. Self-knowledge, particularly for the researcher of the spirit, means knowing the limits of our abilities. We can train ourselves in self-knowledge in the way described in my above-mentioned book, and then we will be able to distinguish between our own feeling and will and the external feeling and will entering them from the spiritual world. We will reach the stage where not being able to tell the difference between our own feeling and willing and that from outside will seem as absurd as not being able to distinguish between hunger and bread. Everyone knows where hunger stops and bread begins; just as everyone knows that hunger itself does not make bread appear — desirable as this would be from a social standpoint. True self-knowledge enables us to differentiate between the hunger of our own feeling and willing and what comes to meet them from the spiritual world (as hunger is met with bread). Once the outside feeling and will have penetrated our own, the two will continue to exist in us side by side.

In my case, the close relationship between my feeling and willing and what I recognized as external feeling and willing fertilized my thinking. As a result, thoughts appeared in my mind as gifts of the external feeling and willing and solved the original problem of investigating a certain historical epoch.

What happens there in our spiritual experience runs counter to a similar process in the physical world. When we meet people in the physical world and get together with them, we first see them, then speak to them, and exchange ideas. The opposite happens in the spiritual experience I have described; there we observe thoughts in ourselves and have the feeling that a foreign feeling and will are present. Then we perceive a separate spiritual individuality as a real, separate being, but one that lives only in the spiritual world. Then, we gradually get to know this individuality in a reverse process to meeting someone in physical life. In the spiritual sphere, we approach the individual through the foreign feeling and willing we find within us, and get closer to the personality by being together with it.

I found out that in my case the foreign feeling and willing that fertilized my own thinking came from an individual I had known well and who had been torn from our circle of friends by her death a little more than a year ago.[5] She had died at a relatively early age, in her best mid-life years, and had taken unused life energy into the spiritual worlds. The feeling and willing that entered my own originated in the intensity of this unused life energy. Generally, people live to a ripe old age and use up their vitality during their lifetime. However, if they die relatively young, this strength remains as unused potential and is available to them in the spiritual world. These life forces that were not used in our friend's short life enabled me, because of our friendship, to solve a problem which required her strength.

What I earlier called "the capacity of the inner word" leads to such revelations of the spiritual world as this one of a dead person. At the same time, this capacity allows us to look beyond our life enclosed between birth and death, or between conception and death, and gain insight into human life extending into infinite periods of time through repeated earth lives. Then we can understand the life of those we were very close to, as I was to our dead friend.

As we get to know ourselves or another person through the soul faculties I have described, we discover not only the physical life between birth and death, but the spiritual human being who structures his own body, lives in repeated incarnations on earth, and between each death and new birth in the spiritual world. Now you will easily understand that I could gain deeper insight into the soul-spiritual being of our dead friend because she stood before my soul as a spiritual being.

The process of getting to know another being in the spiritual world is the reverse of that in the physical realm. At first, we learn how to be together spiritually with the other being, and then we come to know the being itself as a spiritual being. And then entering the spiritual world becomes a reality.

To return to our example, it became clear that during an earlier incarnation in the first Christian centuries, the friend whom we knew in her short life here had taken in much of that Christian culture. However, she had not been able to digest it all because of the restrictions of the time, and entered this life with the undigested material. It burst the confines of this incarnation, but remained present as life energy. And now through my connection with her, I was blessed with insight into the period my work was concerned with, the age in which our friend had lived in a past incarnation.

It doesn't matter that many people in our age make fun of what I have just described and belittle an attitude that guides us thus into the spiritual world. If you have developed yourself along these paths, you know that when you accomplished something you could not possibly have done by yourself, it was because specific spiritual beings helped you. In addition, your view of the world will expand because you will know that you cannot expect hunger to produce bread, and because you know that the power of spiritual beings has entered into your own abilities. As our view into the sphere of the dead widens, our insight into the spiritual world also deepens through the methods I have described and finally encompasses concrete events and beings that are just as real as the physical world around us.

People do not mind our talking about the spiritual world in general terms; they admit there is a spiritual realm behind the sensory one. But they are less tolerant if we talk about concrete beings in the spiritual world whom we perceive just as we do beings of the mineral, plant, animal, and human kingdoms. However, if we do not shy away from developing our slumbering soul forces, we find that it is just as wrong to talk about the spirit in general terms, or in vague pantheistic terms, as to speak about nature in general terms. For example, if walking across a meadow and looking at flowers, perhaps some day lilies here, violets there, and so on, we would point to them and not say their names but instead just "this is nature, that is nature, and there is nature; everything is nature and more nature" —that is no different from talking about spirit, spirit, and more spirit in a vaguely pantheistic way. We can understand the spiritual world only if we really know the individual beings living there and what happens between them.

In objection to the possibility of knowing the spiritual world people often claim that harboring such fantasies about the realm of the spirit simply runs counter to intelligent behavior in the physical world. Although this conclusion seems justified on the basis of the capacities of human intelligence, it can be sustained only as long as one is ignorant of the extensive power of the intellect, that is, the power of human thinking, as we can know it through spiritual research.

To return to our example, imagine someone has the task to develop certain ideas here on earth. He learns how to encounter a spiritual being, in this case, a dead person who adds his or her thinking — now modified by the spiritual world almost into willing that thinks and thinking that feels — to the human individual's thinking and feeling. The intelligent ideas the dead individual wants to produce emerge in the human being on earth. The deceased possesses feeling and willing, just as on earth, as well as other soul capacities not developed on earth. Therefore, the dead have the desire to connect their thinking and feeling with human thoughts. That is why they unite with the person on earth. As the thinking, feeling, and willing of the dead penetrate the living person, ideas are stimulated. Thus, the dead can experience these ideas, something they could not do on their own. That is why they communicate with human beings on earth. However, this communication and stimulation of ideas is possible only if our thinking has been freed from the nervous system and the brain, that is, if we have developed thinking independent of the brain.

As we liberate our thinking from the body, we feel as though our thinking were snatched away from us, as though it expanded and spread out in space and time. Thinking, which we normally say takes place inside us, unites with the surrounding spiritual world, streams into it and achieves a certain autonomy from us similar to the relative independence of the eyes, which are set in their sockets rather like autonomous organs. Thus, although our liberated thinking is connected with our higher self, it is so independent as to act as our spiritual organ of perception for the thoughts and feelings of other spiritual beings. Its function is thus similar to that of our eyes. Gradually, the thinking processes, normally limited by our intelligence, become independent from our being as spiritual organs of perception.

To put it differently, what we experience subjectively, what is comprised by our intelligence, namely, our outer thinking, is nothing but shadowy entities, thought entities, mere ideas reflecting external things. When thinking becomes clairvoyant and separates from brain and nervous system, it begins to develop inner activity, a life of its own, and to stream out, as our own experience, into the spiritual world. In a sense, we send the tendrils of our clairvoyant thinking out into the spiritual realm and, as they become immersed in this world, they perceive the will that feels and feeling that wills of the other beings in that realm.

After what we have said about self-knowledge as a necessity on the path of spiritual development — and from this it follows that modesty is a must — allow me to comment on clairvoyant thinking, and please do not think me presumptuous for saying this. When we enliven our thinking through clairvoyant development, it becomes independent and also a very precise and useful tool. True clairvoyance increases the precision, accuracy, and logical power of our thinking. As a result, we can use it with more exactness and close adaptation to its subject; our intelligence becomes more practical and more thoroughly structured. Therefore, the clairvoyant can easily understand the scope of ordinary scientific research, whereas conventional science requires bringing out . . . [text missing] of the mind. It is easy to see why modern natural science cannot comprehend the findings of clairvoyant research, but those who have developed true clairvoyance can comprehend the full significance of the achievements of the natural sciences. There can be no question, therefore, of spiritual science opposing conventional science; the other way around is more likely. Only clairvoyant development can organize the power of the mind, making it inwardly independent, alive, comprehensible. That is why the materialistic way of thinking cannot penetrate to the logic that gives us the certainty that clairvoyant knowledge really does lead to perception of the spiritual world.

The example of my clairvoyant experiences with a dead person shows that intelligence and thinking are specific qualities of souls living in a physical body, of human beings on earth. The deceased wanted to connect herself with a human being so that what lived in her in a completely different, supersensible way could take the form of intelligent thoughts. The dead individual and the living person were thinking their thoughts together in the head of the latter, as it were.

As specifically human qualities, intellect and thinking can be developed only in human beings on earth, and they allow even people who are not clairvoyant to understand the results of clairvoyant research. You see, our independent thinking becomes the spiritual eye, as it were, for the perception of the spiritual world. Supersensible research, which uses this spiritual eye for clairvoyant thinking, has found that this eye is active, that the spiritual feelers are put out in all directions, but our physical eyes only passively allow impressions to come to them. When we as spiritual researchers have taken the revelations of the supersensible world into our thinking, they continue to live in our thoughts. We can then tell other people about what we have taken pains to bring into our living thought processes, and they can understand us if they do not allow materialistic prejudices to get in the way.

There is a sort of inner language in the human soul that normally remains silent. But when concepts enter the soul, which the spiritual researcher acquires by allowing his or her will and feeling to be stimulated by the spiritual world and its beings, this language responds immediately with an echoing sound. Careful and thorough study of spiritual science will gradually silence the objection that the spiritual researcher's reports of the realm of the spirit can only be believed because they cannot really be understood. People will see that human intelligence is indeed able to understand information from the spiritual world, but only if it is the result of true spiritual experiences and true spiritual research. They will realize that it is wrong to say human intelligence does not suffice to comprehend revelations from the spiritual world and that therefore they have to be accepted on authority. They will come to know that the only obstacle to such understanding is to have preconceived notions and prejudices.

Eventually, people will treat information from the spiritual world as they treat the insights of, say, astronomy, biology, physics, and chemistry. That is, even if they are not astronomers, biologists, physicists, or chemists, they accept the scientists' findings about the physical world on the basis of a natural feeling for truth, which we may call a silent language of the soul.

The harmony between intelligence and clairvoyance will become much more obvious, and then people will admit that clairvoyant research approaches the world of spiritual beings and processes with the same attitude that also motivates the natural sciences. In view of the considerable opposition to spiritual science, it will comfort us to know that our modern culture will eventually come to the point Giordano Bruno did. Looking up to the blue vault of the sky, which people then considered to exist exactly as they perceived it, Bruno declared that they saw the blue dome of the sky only because that was as far as their vision reached. They themselves in a way imposed that limit; in reality space extends into infinity. The limits people saw so clearly, based on the illusion of their senses, were created by the limitation of their vision.

You see, now and in the future, the spiritual researcher will have to stand up before the world and say that there is also a firmament with regard to time, the time between birth and death. We perceive this firmament of time through the illusion of the senses. In fact, we create it ourselves because our spiritual vision is limited, just as in earlier times people "created" the blue firmament of space. Space extends endlessly beyond the blue dome of the sky, and time also continues infinitely beyond the boundaries of birth and death. Our own infinite spiritual life is embedded in this infinite time together with the rest of spiritual life in the world.

The time will come when people will realize that clairvoyant research strengthens and deepens our intelligence, producing a more subtle and refined logic. Such improved understanding will silence many, seemingly justified, current opinions on spiritual science claiming that the philosophical writings of several authors prove that our cognitive and intellectual capacities are limited. After all, aren't the reasons these philosophers present to prove the limits of human cognition convincing? Are they not logical? How can researchers of spiritual science hope to refute these convincing, logical arguments for the limits of our capacity to know?

The time will come when people will see the lack of substance and precision in such logic, when they will understand that something can be irrefutably correct as philosophical argument, and yet be completely refuted by life. After all, before the discovery of the microscope or the telescope people might very well have "irrefutably" proven that human eyes can never see a cell. Still, human ingenuity invented the microscope and the telescope, which increased the power of our eyes. Similarly, life has outdistanced the irrefutable proof of the philosophers. Life does not need to refute the arguments of this or that philosopher. Their proofs may be indisputable, but the reality of life must progress beyond them by strengthening our cognitive capacity and spiritual understanding through spiritual instruments.

In the present state of our culture with its prevailing belief in the incontrovertibility of the philosophers' proofs, these things are not generally or readily accepted. However, as our culture continues to develop, it will reach a higher logic than the one supporting these proofs of purely external philosophy. This higher logic will be one of life, of life of the spirit, of insights based on spiritual science. A time will come when people, while still respecting the accomplishments and discoveries of the natural sciences as much as we do now, will nevertheless realize that for our inner life these marvelous achievements have brought more questions than answers. If you study biology, astronomy, and so on, you will see that they have reached their limits. Do these sciences provide answers? No, they are really only raising questions. The answers will come from what stands behind the subject matter of the natural sciences. The answers will come from the sources of clairvoyant research.

To summarize, let me repeat that the world extends beyond the realm of the senses, and behind the sensory world we find spirit. In spiritual science, the spirit reveals itself to clairvoyant perception, and it is only then that we can see the divine nature of the magnificent sensory world around us. The world is vast, and the spirit is the necessary counterbalance to the physical world. A proper perspective on our future cultural development reveals that in trying to understand the world in its entirety, people will strive not for a one-sided exploration of the natural world, as many now assume. Instead, people will seek to unite science, intellect, and clairvoyant research. Only in this union will people truly come to understand themselves and their own spirit. Only then will they realize solutions to the world's future riddles, never to be solved completely, and feel satisfaction in that knowledge.

Those who have taken the true impulse of spiritual science to heart can sense even now in our culture the yearning and the latent urge in many souls to go beyond the immediate and sensory in science. Through use and inner assimilation of the capacities the sciences have created in recent centuries, these souls long to be strengthened so that they can live in the spiritual worlds from where alone can come true satisfaction for the human soul.

APPENDIX

The following two lectures differ in character and content from the preceding five. In both, Rudolf Steiner approaches the central theme from a much wider perspective. In addition, "Faith and Knowledge" is not a complete, word for word, record of a lecture but notes summarizing what Steiner said. Therefore, the two lectures have been placed in the appendix.

LECTURE SIX

FAITH AND KNOWLEDGE

Notes from a lecture given in Prague, April 17, 1914

Given the large amount of literature available, it is always possible to learn about the findings of spiritual science, particularly when anthroposophical groups work together. Since we are together now, I would like to discuss some guiding ideas out of spiritual impulses, ideas that continue in a more esoteric way what we spoke about more generally in yesterday's public lecture.[1]

Many people today still believe in the contrast between faith and knowledge, faith and cognition. They say science can tell us about the world outside us, the only one we can know of with certainty. However, concerning the spiritual world, we must have faith. This attitude appears to contradict spiritual science, which strives to give us real knowledge of and insight into the spiritual world. In fact, it has to enter souls in our time in just this form, as insight and knowledge. In earlier incarnations our souls were in a completely different condition than now. They were more primitive, but in those times there were great individuals and many people connected with them. Those individuals conveyed ideas of the spiritual world, which we can still find in certain tribes and peoples and trace to individuals such as Hermes, Zarathustra, Moses, Buddha, and Krishna.[2] Spiritual ideas had to be poured into people's souls.

In the physical world life is not just toil and work, but slaving and drudgery. Most of this toil and work is not in the sense of "it's been a hard day's work," but in the sense of unconscious occurrences caused by our thinking — in fact, our whole soul life as it takes its course.

We are all much more alike when we are born than we think. We do not resemble each other in our appearance, but in our structure. The forces at work in a child are active at an unconscious level. The spirit takes hold of the body and structures it. Only then does the sculpting and elaborating of the nerves begin. This happens independently of our mind, at a time when we are not yet able to use it. Then we become aware of ourselves as an I. That is when the wisdom we have brought with us from the gods, from the spiritual world, ceases.

In the first period after birth, we have only life forces, so to speak; our life then is nothing but a continuation of the spiritual world. Death in infancy is due to external bodily causes, and the child's soul plays no part in it.

Then we begin to deplete our physical bodies with every thought, every feeling. We must sleep to make up for what we have depleted during the day. If we did not thus eat away at our physical organization, we would have a budding and burgeoning life. Our etheric body always wants to bud and to sprout, but the astral body needs to consume what the etheric body builds up, and thus suppresses it. When we are sleeping, compensation for what has been eaten away and killed off flows into us from the spiritual world to reestablish the balance. The normal amount of sleep replaces exactly as much as has been depleted. If we decided to sleep more, as some retired people do, we would sleep too much. Of course, that is no objection to sleeping a lot. Since intellectual work takes a lot out of our physical organization, people doing that kind of work need much sleep. But if we sleep too much, we have too many new life forces and these then begin to proliferate; the human being then abounds with life forces. This surplus of life forces leads to illness. So if we want to do more than merely make up for what we depleted through our daily work and advance spiritually, we have to consciously take what we need from the spiritual world.

The founders of our religions believed it was their task to lead their people, to use up life forces, which will then be compensated for. However, what has to develop within us for the progress of humanity must be consciously drawn from the spiritual world so that it will not die in our physical existence.

That is why the founders of our religions provided ideas they had received from the spiritual world. These truly spiritual thoughts nourish our soul and maintain it. It would be the death of our soul if it always had to live in thoughts taken only from the physical world. In earlier times, religious beliefs were such spiritual thoughts human souls need. That phase of our development has been completed, and we live now in a time when we on earth will gradually lose the ability to take in what speaks only to our emotions, our faith. We can still preserve this faith for a time, galvanizing it, so to speak, but we cannot keep it for the future. The principle "I believe" has to be replaced with "I believe what I know." People will begin to feel that this new principle must be applied. Otherwise we deny ourselves any possibility of knowing something about the life between death and a new birth. Then we would return to pitiful conditions in our next incarnation. Enthusiasm for other ideals, all clearly justified, is certainly a good thing and has to exist. However, in comparison with the foundations of spiritual science, these ideals cannot be put into practice directly. Lacking its knowledge, they can only be precursors of spiritual science.

As we progress in our spiritual research, we will feel the need to remain silent rather than to speak. If we speak nevertheless, it is out of insight into the conditions necessary for our time. Knowledge alone will make us free, and it is the task of the future to win the freedom of the human soul.

Thoughts of great spiritual power came from the founders of our religions. They were thoughts of faith that could wonderfully illuminate the region beyond death. These ideas were transformed into a true, spiritual light that revealed the environment beyond death to human beings. But the time will come when we will have to live in freedom. And even if new religious leaders were still to proclaim the old teachings of faith with the voice and the power of the gods, we would no longer understand them. We are experiencing this now. The sciences concerned with the outer world have arrived, as they had to. A great contemporary scientist, Max Müller, said that if an angel were to come down and proclaim news of the spiritual world, people would not understand or believe him.[3]

That is the development of humanity. It seems to lead inevitably to the loss of our ability to imbue ourselves with thoughts related to the spiritual worlds. That would mean we would have less light after death to illuminate our spiritual environment by ourselves. After all, no sun will shine from the outside on the world around us then, the light has to come from us. *We* then take the place of the sun and illuminate our surroundings after death. People unable to do this will have to return and repeat life on earth to assimilate thoughts and ideas that are fruitful for their existence after death. When we understand this, more than the usual enthusiasm for spreading spiritual science will loosen our tongue and prompt us to speak. Believing in what we know — that will be the need of humanity in the future.

In ancient times, religious ideas, myths, and fairy tales gave souls light for the spiritual world. It is easy to say that myths and fairy tales developed in the childhood stages of the human race. Of course, people did not physically meet the angels that myths and fairy tales speak about. But thinking based on philosophy will be of little use in the spiritual world where such knowledge has no meaning. It is easy to say fairy tales are not based on truth. Spiritual researchers are not so naive, and know that fiery dragons do not really fly through the air. However, they always knew it was necessary to form the Imagination of the fiery dragon, for when it lives in the soul, it casts light on the spiritual world. These are powerful Imaginations. That is the principle behind all myths; they are not intended to reflect external reality accurately, but to enable us to live in the spiritual world.

Materialists say myths and fairy tales originated in the childhood stage of the human race. But in its childhood, humanity was taught by the gods. In the process of our evolution, myths and fairy tales are gradually lost, but children should not grow up without them. It makes a tremendous difference whether or not children are allowed to grow up with fairy tales. The power of the fairy tale images, which give wings to the soul, becomes apparent only at a later age. Growing up without fairy tales leads later to boredom, to world-weariness. Indeed, it can even cause physical symptoms — fairy tales can help to prevent illnesses. The qualities that seep into our soul from fairy tales later emerge as a zest for life, enthusiasm for being alive, and an ability to cope with life, all of which can be seen even in old age. Children have to experience the power of the content of fairy tales while they are young and can still do so. People who cannot live with ideas that have no reality on the physical plane will be dead to the spiritual world. Philosophies based only on the material world are the death of our soul. Physical evolution leads to the death of the spiritual world. We must reach a view of the world based not on appearances, but resting solidly on its own inherent structure. We have to move toward the principle: I believe what I know.

We have to learn to pay attention to the symptoms of our cultural life. For example, I once gave a lecture in a town in southern Germany, and afterward two Catholic priests came up to me and said that I was only speaking to educated people, while they spoke so everyone could understand them. In reality, the opposite is the case. Anthroposophy can reach everyone provided we find the way to the simple, ordinary people. The farmer would understand it much better than the so-called educated person if only the way were not blocked by social conventions. In these matters, we must be able to leave ourselves completely out of the picture and not ask what we think best. Instead, we must ask what human souls require in a given era. So I replied to the priests that while their feeling tells them they speak to everyone, the facts will tell them they do not, because not everyone comes to hear them. And it is to those who do not come to them that I speak.

On earth we gain knowledge and insight through our physical and etheric bodies. Let us examine carefully how much of what is in our soul comes from the physical world. Light, for example, reaches us through the eyes. The process of seeing is one of deterioration right from its start in the eyes. The deterioration starts directly at the retina. The process detaches itself from life. In the morning, after sleep, our eyes have been restored and are filled with pure life. However, as we perceive, something forms in the living tissue that is no longer alive but only mineral. And we perceive the outer world, which is mirrored in us, because this process continues in the nerve tissue. Thus, insofar as the physical body is the bearer of these processes, it is not alive.

The etheric body is the bearer of thoughts that are also mirror images. People could easily discover that our thoughts reflect the supersensible. Thoughts will never lend themselves to inspection under the microscope because in reality they live in the etheric body. They are formed by our thinking, which is mirrored in the physical body. We can see from this that understanding and knowledge are dependent on the physical and etheric bodies, which are affected only by the impressions of the physical world. Completely different thoughts have to take hold in our soul, in our astral body, and all our feeling, willing, and thinking not limited to the physical plane. Otherwise we will remain inwardly dead. All thoughts that represent objects are meaningful only on the physical plane. This is implied in the very question, "Are thoughts that do not represent objects justified?" Only with the thoughts living freely in the spirit, living freely in the astral body and the I can we gain insight, only with those thoughts can we live. These thoughts not only represent things, but are also inwardly active and alive; they create something out of themselves and out of us.

In modern art, naturalism predominates these days. In ancient times the soul was filled with images that brought activity into the thoughts of the astral body. Everything depicting only outer things is meaningless in the spiritual world. We must imbue ourselves with new images that can once again meaningfully permeate our soul. Often we take hold of something we believe to exist only in our imagination, to be only fantasy. This is frequently only a memory of something originating on the physical plane. We can revitalize what would otherwise die in our soul only by enlivening our images with thoughts that do not originate on the physical level and are not created by that kind of imagination.

People increasingly misuse the phrase: A beautiful soul in a beautiful body, a healthy soul in a healthy body. This phrase was appropriate for the understanding of earlier times. Unfortunately, today it is seen as a statement of cause; if someone has a healthy body, people conclude that a healthy soul lives in it. Whatever makes the body healthy will do the same for the soul.

If people do not develop thoughts that keep the astral body inwardly agile, they will suffer from mineral deposits even in childhood and as a result become ill later in life. And the world they enter after death will remain dark, because they do not radiate any light themselves. The rays of the sun strike a surface and that is how we see things. But in the spiritual world we are the source of light; we illuminate the surroundings we are supposed to see. Souls feeling the need to pursue spiritual science may not be aware of these circumstances, but they live in the depths of the soul. Just as in the physical world sunlight comes from the outside, so we must make ourselves sunlike in the spiritual world. We have to light in ourselves the spiritual fuel, the inner flame, to illuminate the realm of the spirit.

Physicists imagine the red of a rose can be traced to oscillation, to variations in wavelength. People say there is really no sound, only vibrations of air. They claim what we hear as sound exists only in our ears. Well, a simple experiment can teach us otherwise, namely, if we have someone wake us up by knocking on the door. We will notice that we were not conscious during the night when we were asleep, but that on waking up we were already living in the knocking. We ourselves have to enter into the knocking sound. We use the other person to do the knocking because our soul itself cannot do it. If we resolved firmly to wake up, we could do so, but this way we are only using the other person as a tool.

If materialist views continue to persist for several generations more, the red of roses will really disappear. People will actually see little gray atoms vibrating as an atomic whirl, not because they have to see them or because they exist, but because they will have trained themselves to see them. That is why it is necessary to spread spiritual science, to prevent having to live in a future filled with nothing other than physical atoms swirling around.

We are not talking about the physical ether but the one that is living thought. We must realize first of all that a rose is not a mass of whirling atoms, but that behind it there are real living and interweaving elemental beings. The theory of the spiritual world is secondary; the main thing is to concentrate our feeling, to feel ourselves living and weaving in our new perception of the reality of the spiritual world. This is the resurrection of the spiritual world in our souls, the truly ecumenical Easter event.

Our ancestors required a different event that was connected to the time when the sun reaches its zenith. When everything in nature was budding and blossoming, they experienced an ecstasy that reaffirmed for them the existence of the spiritual world. What they experienced then at St. John's tide we now have to experience in the spring, at Easter. We have to be able to celebrate the awakening of the soul, the resurrection of the soul, when spiritual science speaks to us not merely as a theory, but as living knowledge.

LECTURE SEVEN

ROBERT HAMERLING: POET AND THINKER

Berlin, April 26, 1914

On July 15, 1889, I was standing in the St. Leonhard cemetery near Graz with the writer Rosegger and the sculptor Hans Brandstetter as the body of the Austrian poet Robert Hamerling was lowered into the grave.[1] Robert Hamerling had been called from the physical plane a few days earlier. He died after decades of unutterable suffering that grew to an unbearable level at the end of his life. Prior to the burial, the body had been laid out in the beautiful Stifting House on the outskirts of the Austro-Styrian town of Graz. The physical form left behind by his great soul lay there, a wonderful reflection of a life of striving to reach the highest levels of the spirit: so expressive, so eloquent was this physical form. It also bore the imprint of the unspeakable suffering this poet had had to endure in his life!

On that occasion a little girl of ten could be seen among the closest mourners. She was Robert Hamerling's ward and had brightened and cheered the poet's last years with the promise of her character. She was the girl to whom Robert Hamerling had dedicated the lines that fundamentally reveal his mood in the last years of his life.[2] And because they let us see so deeply into Hamerling's soul, please permit me to read you these lines:

To B.(ertha)

Child, like a butterfly harmlessly
Fluttering past the pain-racked invalid,
When having seen me begin the homeward journey,
In the wake of suffering
Do not think of me in your flush of youth:
A fleeting thought is all that you would give;
Nor when happily in love, in marriage or in
  motherhood:
Your memory would be only a pale reflection in
  the bustle of your life.
Only at sixty years of age, please think of me:
The poor sick man you saw
Year after year stretched on a bed of suffering,
Who, tortured by unceasing pain,
Spoke little, save laborious groans;
Nothing was he to you and nothing could he be.
At sixty years of age, child, think of him:
Then you will muse on him, muse long,
And late, deep compassion will rise in you
For him then long at rest from suffering.
A teardrop fills your eye as offering
For him long paled in death,
Who nothing was to you, and nothing could be.

It is not necessary to describe the situation of a poet who could write lines that speak so powerfully of his suffering in virtually the entire second half of his life. There was much gossip, even after Hamerling had already been confined to his bed for a large part of his life, and allegations about the sybaritic life the author of "Ahasver" supposedly led. It was even rumored that he lived in a sumptuous house in Graz, and that he had a large number of girls for his pleasure, who had to perform Greek dances day after day and other such things. All these stories were told at a time when illness kept him laid up while the sun was shining outside. He was forced to stay in bed in his small room, knowing that outside the sun was shining on the meadows, on the glorious nature he had enjoyed so much in the brief periods he was able to leave his sickbed.

And this same bright sun was shining gloriously when we accompanied the deceased to his last resting place on July 15, 1889. There are few indeed who lived under such outward constraints and yet were devoted with every fiber of their soul to what is great, beautiful, monumental, magnificent, and joyous in the world.

I remember one time sitting with a young musician in Vienna who was a great friend of Hamerling's. This young man was essentially a poor fellow who soon succumbed to a mental illness. He was deeply pessimistic and never tired of complaining about life. And since he loved Hamerling a great deal, he loved to cite the poet in his complaints about life. On this occasion, the young musician once again wanted to quote Hamerling as a pessimist. As we were sitting together in a café, I was able to call for a newspaper that contained a small occasional poem by Hamerling entitled "Personal Request." I showed it to the young musician.

Personal Request

Say that I write bad verses,
Say that I steal the silverware,
Say I'm a rotten German
Because my diet says
I can't eat Jews
And Slavs for breakfast;
Or that I betray our Austria

Because I sing the praise of Bismarck.
Say that I'm stricken with grief because
Praise for me is sadly lacking,
Slandered I am basely on occasion —
But I ask one thing only:
Do not say that I'm a *pessimist,*
That the last word in my singing
Belongs to blasé-modern
Stupid, dull unhappiness with living!
What? The poet is a pessimist
Because he makes complaining noises?
Just because the world is lovely
And life seems so charming to him
He would painfully regret it
If his part he were to forfeit.
If you call pessimists all persons
Who complain, then pessimistic
Is the man from whom a cry
Escapes while he is at the dentist!
Everything the critics say, believe them,
Except that I'm a pessimist!
I hate this word. To me it smells
Rather like its final syllable.[3]

These words characterize Hamerling's attitude and show that he lived in greatest pain (he wrote as much to Rosegger) at the time of writing this poem "Personal Request." He wrote to Rosegger: "I am not worried about becoming a pessimist, but I do fear going mad or becoming an imbecile, as sometimes I can manage only a few minutes respite from the never-ending pain!"[4] The man who began his poetic career with words truly sounding like a lifetime's program was worried about going mad or becoming an imbecile, but not about becoming a pessimist. For when Robert Hamerling sent his first major poem, "Venus in Exile," out into the world, he gave it the motto:

> Go on your way, a holy messenger,
> And sing in joyful tones
> Of the dawning day,
> Of the realm of beauty to come.

That was his attitude throughout his life. We must recall one very memorable scene if we want to fully understand Hamerling's unique nature. A few months or weeks before his death, he moved from his flat in Graz — where he lived on the street then called Realschulstrasse; now it is Hamerlingstrasse — to a small summer house, called Stifting House, situated in a secluded area on the outskirts of the town. Two servants had to carry the invalid down; his flat was three floors up. Several times he almost fainted. But on either side of him he had a parcel tied up with a broad ribbon, which went round his neck like a stole; they contained the wrapped manuscript of his last work, *The Atomistic Will.*[5] This was characteristic of the way this poet lived and of what he loved. He did not want the manuscript of this philosophical work to leave his hands for even a minute! He was so ill that two servants had to carry him down; yet he had to hold on to the thing that filled his life. So he was carried down and taken out to Stifting House in the most beautiful sunshine, sighing, "Oh, what pleasure to ride like this; if only I were less ill, less ill!"

The soul and spirit at work under these physical conditions remained open to all that is great and beautiful, all that is filled with spirit in the world. It worked out of the wellsprings of greatness, beauty, and spirituality in such a way that we cannot really be surprised by his attitude to pessimism. We cannot be surprised to see in Hamerling's spirit living cosmic evidence that the spiritual forces in us can triumph over material and natural forces, however obstructive they may be, in every situation.

Fifty-nine years earlier, that is in 1830, Robert Hamerling was born in Austria in an area called Waldviertel.[6] Because of its special natural configuration that region is eminently suited — and was probably more so then than now when it is crisscrossed by railroad lines — to concentrate the soul inwardly if it is awake and to deepen the soul. The Waldviertel region is basically a backwater of civilization, although someone was born and lived there in the first half of the nineteenth century who was also widely known in Austria this side of the river Leitha. He has probably been forgotten by now, and at most continues to live in the memory of the people in the Waldviertel, in numerous folk legends. I have to add that I often heard tell of this person's fame because my parents came from the Waldviertel area. Thus, I could at least hear about the remnants of his peculiar fame, which is characteristic of the atmosphere of cultural isolation in that region. This famous person was none other than one of the "most famous" robbers and murderers of the time, namely, Grasel. This Grasel was certainly more famous than anyone else who came from the Waldviertel region.

In his later years, Hamerling wrote about the Waldviertel area, and I want to read you just a few lines from what he said about his native region where he lived for the first ten or fifteen years of his life, because I believe these words can throw much greater light on Hamerling's nature than any academic characterization. He writes:

> I do not know how much the construction of a railroad skirting the Waldviertel area has affected the latter's isolation from the world. In 1867, the appearance of a stranger still created quite a stir there. If such a person came along on foot or by coach, the oxen plowing the

> fields came to a halt and turned their heads to gawk at the new apparition. The farmer made one or two feeble attempts to drive them on with his whip — but in vain, and finally, he did likewise, and the plow rested until the stranger had disappeared behind the next hill or forest. That, too, is the image of an idyllic atmosphere![7]

Hamerling's life and personality are an example of a soul growing out of and beyond its environment, and of an individuality's development. He was the son of a poor weaver. Since they were completely impoverished, his parents were evicted from their home at a time when Hamerling was not yet capable of even saying "I." His father was forced to go abroad while his mother remained in the Waldviertel area, in Schönau, with the young boy. There the child experienced the beauties of the Waldviertel region. A scene from that time remained always in his memory of an experience he believed actually gave him his own being. The seven-year-old boy was going down a hill. It was evening, and the sun was setting in the west. Something came toward him, golden, out of the golden sunshine, and Hamerling describes what was shining forth in the golden light as follows:

> Among the most significant memories of my boyhood, but also most difficult to convey, are the often strange moods that passed through my soul when I was a roaming boy. In part they came from the moment's lively impressions and stimulation, usually from nature around me, in part they were waking dreams and premonitions. Speaking about himself, the mystic Jakob Böhme used to say that the higher meaning, the mystical life of the spirit was awakened in him miraculously at the moment when he was dreamily absorbed in gazing at a pewter bowl sparkling in the sunlight.[8] Perhaps every spiritual

> person has a pewter bowl like Böhme's as the origin of his real inner awakening. I vividly recall a certain evening when I was about seven years old. I was going down a hill, and the sunset shone toward me like a miracle, a spiritual vision. It filled my heart with an unforgettably strange mood, with a presentiment that today seems to me like a calling, reflecting my future destiny. In high spirits, I hurried toward an unknown destination; yet, at the same time my soul was filled with a melancholy that made me want to cry. If that moment could have been explained out of the surrounding circumstances, if it had not been so completely unique, it would surely not have remained so indelibly in my memory.[9]

Thus, in the poet's seventh year the poetic and spiritual muse drew near. At that time, the seed for everything that was later to become of this soul was laid into it from out of the cosmos, so to speak. The nice thing is that Hamerling ascribes his poetic calling to such an event, as if it were a miracle the cosmos itself performed on him.

Because of his parents' poverty, the boy had to be educated at the Cistercian monastery of Zwettl.[10] In return for his school lessons, he had to sing in the monastery choir. At that time, Hamerling was between ten and fourteen years old. He formed a close relationship to a strange personality at the monastery, namely, Father Hugo Traumihler, a person completely given over to mystical contemplation and a strict ascetic life. At that time the boy already possessed a thirst for the beauty of the cosmos and an urge to deepen his soul. You can imagine that he was inspired by the inner experiences Father Traumihler described from his inner contemplation of the secrets of the heart and soul. He was a mystic of a very elementary, primitive kind who nevertheless made a deep impression on Hamerling's soul.

But it is impossible to talk about the poet Hamerling without mentioning what was such a great part of his longing: the longing to be a great human being. When he returned on a trip to the Waldviertel long after he had left the area, people who knew that he came from there asked him what he wanted to be.[11] But although he was already well past twenty, Hamerling had not thought about what he wanted to be. This realization brought it home to him that at that age you cannot avoid the question "What do you want to do?" The only thing he could tell himself was: "Well, I cannot really tell them what I want to be, because they would not understand. For when I am asked what I want to be, I want to answer: I want to become a human being!" So sometimes he said he wanted to be a philologist or an astronomer or something like that. People could understand that. But they would not have understood that someone who had finished his studies might intend to become a human being.

Well, much could be said about the development of Hamerling as a poet and, above all, about the unfolding of three things in his soul. The first he later described in *The Atomistic Will* by saying that the Greeks called the universe "cosmos," a word connected with beauty.[12] That, to him, was characteristic of the Greek spirit, for his soul was filled with the beauty that resonates throughout the universe. And his heart's desire was to see humankind in turn permeated by that beauty; that was what he wanted to express in poetic form. So everything in him strove toward beauty, toward the beauty-filled world of the Greeks. Yet he saw so many aspects of life that cast a pall over the beauty intended by nature. For him beauty was identical with spirituality. He would often survey everything he knew about Hellenism and then look with sadness at modern culture, the readers of his poetry. He wanted to write poetry for this modern culture in order to fill it with sounds that would encourage people to bring beauty and spirituality back into life, and thus return happiness to life on earth. Hamerling found it impossible to speak of a discrepancy between the world and beauty in human life. He was inspired by the belief that life should be infused with beauty, that beauty should be alive in the world, and from his youth on he would have preferred to live for that alone. It was like an instinct in his soul. But he had met with much that showed him the modern age must struggle through many things that frustrate our ideals in life.

Hamerling was a student in 1848. He was a member of the liberation movement and was arrested by the police for this "great crime" and given a special punishment, as happened to many who had been part of the liberation movement in Vienna at that time. If they went beyond what the police thought permissible, they were taken to the barber where their hair was cut as a sign that they were "democrats." These days you no longer risk having your hair cut just because you hold liberal views — progress indeed! The other thing not allowed at that time was the wearing of a broad-brimmed hat. This again was taken as a sign of liberal views. One had to wear a so-called "topper," a top hat, which had full police approval.

Hamerling had to put up with this and much else. Let me just mention one more event as a small indication of how the world treated the great poet; I believe it leads to a much better characterization than an abstract description. The event I am referring to happened when Hamerling had concluded his years at university and was about to take his teaching examination. He had good grades in Greek, Latin, and mathematics. Indeed, he received excellent grades on his Greek and Latin. But if we read further in his report card, we find that although Hamerling claimed to have read some grammar books, his performance in the examination did not indicate a thorough study of the German language.

This was said of the man who has enriched the German language so immeasurably through his unique style!

I would like to draw your attention to another experience Hamerling had. In 1851, he became acquainted with a family and one evening was invited to stay for a party. He would have gladly joined them, but he could not stay. Then the daughter of the family had a glass of punch sent over to his student quarters. What were his feelings then? He suddenly had the urge to take pencil and paper, and he felt himself transported into another world. At first he saw images of world history, presented as if in a large tableau. Then these images were transformed into a chaos of blossoms, rot, blood, newts, golden fruits, blue eyes, harp music, destruction of life, the thunder of cannons, and quarreling people. Historical scenes alternated with blossoms and salamanders. Then, as if crystallizing from out of the whole, a pale, serious figure with penetrating eyes appeared. At the sight of this figure, Hamerling came to. He looked at the piece of paper. The paper, blank before the vision, had written on it the name Ahasver and below, the outline for the poem "Ahasver."

Hamerling's interest in everything that moves the human soul to its heights and depths was of rare profundity, and combined with a drunkenness with beauty, so to speak. That is why the ten years he spent teaching high school in Trieste on the glorious Adriatic and taking his vacations in neighboring Venice may be described as a happy time for him. He got to know Venice so well that years later he still knew all the nooks and crannies and little alleys where he had walked many times on beautiful evenings. There he saw radiant nature and southern beauty, for which his soul had such a yearning. This southern beauty blossomed in "Greeting in Song from the Adriatic." Like his early works, this poem shows Hamerling's extraordinary talent. It was followed by "Venus in Exile." Hamerling conceived of Venus not only as the embodiment of earthly love, but as the bearer of the beauty that rules and holds sway in the cosmos, a beauty that is in exile as far as modern humanity is concerned. Robert Hamerling's longing as a poet was to liberate beauty and love from their exile. Hence the motto I read to you:

> Go on your way, a holy messenger,
> And sing in joyful tones
> Of the dawning day,
> Of the realm of beauty to come.

But Hamerling's soul could not sing of the "dawning day, / Of the realm of beauty to come" without looking into all the dark recesses of the human soul. The vision of Ahasver shows what Robert Hamerling saw in those recesses. It continued to stand before his soul until he found the poetic form for the personality of Ahasver. Ahasver became the thread running through human life as the personification of an individuality who wants to escape life but cannot. This individuality is then contrasted with that of Nero in Rome, a man always seeking life but unable to find it in sensual saturation and therefore eternally searching.

We can see how life's contradictions confronted Hamerling. This becomes even clearer in his poem "The King of Sion" where he describes a person who wants to bring spiritual salvation from lofty heights to his fellow human beings but falls prey to human weaknesses in the process, to sensuality and so on. Hamerling was always reflecting on the proximity of opposites in life, and he wanted to give this poetic form. Greece arose before his soul in the form to which he wanted to restore it. In *Aspasia*, he described the Greece of his imagination, the country of his yearning, the world of beauty, including the negative aspects such a world of beauty may also bear. In the form of a three-part novel, *Aspasia* became a wonderful poem about cultural history.

Robert Hamerling was not understood, as I learned when I met a man in a godforsaken place whose eyes burned with resentment and whose mouth had an ugly expression. I do not mean physical ugliness, of course; physical ugliness can actually radiate beauty of the highest degree. This man was one of the most vicious critics of *Aspasia*. In comparison with the beauty-filled poet, that man appeared to be one of the ugliest men, and it was clear why his bitter soul could not understand Hamerling.

All of Robert Hamerling's endeavors were of this order. There would be much to tell if I were to recount the whole of his progress through history. He sought to deal with Dante and Robespierre, ending with Homunculus, in whom he wished to embody all of the grotesqueness of modern culture. There would also be much to tell if I were to describe how Hamerling's lyrical muse sought to find the reflective sounds permeating his works in the beauty and colors of nature and in the spirit of nature. Again, there would be much to say if I wanted to give you even just an idea of how Hamerling's lyrical poetry is alive with everything that can comfort our souls regarding the small things in the great ones, or how his poems can give us the invincible faith that the kingdom of beauty will triumph in the human soul however much the demons of discord and ugliness might try to establish their rule. Hamerling's soul suffered in life; yet in the midst of the deepest, most painful suffering, his soul could find joy in the beauty of spiritual activity. His soul could see the discords of the day all around, and yet could immerse itself deeply in the beauty of the night when the starry heavens rose above the waters. Hamerling was able to give meaningful expression to this mood.

I wanted to describe briefly, by means of a few episodes out of Hamerling's life, an image of Robert Hamerling as a poet of the late nineteenth century who was filled with an invincible awareness of the better future of humanity because he was steeped completely in the truth of the beauty of the universe. At the same time, he was a poet who could describe how the spirit can be victorious in us over all the material obstacles and hindrances to our spiritual nature.

It is impossible to understand the poet Hamerling without reference to his lifelong effort to answer the question: How do I become a human being? Everything he created has human greatness, though not always poetic excellence, for Hamerling's stature as a poet is a consequence of his human greatness. When he saw disharmony in life, Hamerling always felt an invincible urge in his soul to find the corresponding harmony, to find the way in which all things ugly must dissolve into beauty when we look at them rightly.

In conclusion, I want to read you a small, insignificant poem typical of Hamerling. In conception and thought it belongs to his early years, but it does characterize the mood, albeit in primitive poetic simplicity, that accompanied him throughout his life:

The Lion and the Rose

On a deep red rose
The angry lion trod
His paw caught fast the thorn
Of this delicate bud.

His paw swelled large;
In angry pain he died.
Refreshed, the red rose drank
The early morning dew.

Be the delicate ever so delicate,
The rough ever so rough,
That which is fragile, gentle, pure —
Beauty, triumphs over all.[13]

This mood — we can see it in everything he wrote —accompanied Hamerling through his life:

Be the delicate ever so delicate,
The rough ever so rough,
That which is fragile, gentle, pure —
Beauty, triumphs over all.

NOTES

LECTURE ONE

1. Rudolf Steiner, *A Road to Self-Knowledge & The Threshold of the Spiritual World,* (London: Rudolf Steiner Press, 1975).

LECTURE TWO

1. Johann Gottlieb Fichte, 1762–1814, German philosopher.
2. In Fichte, *Die Bestimmung des Menschen* ("The Vocation of Man"), vol. 3, section III, Berlin 1800.
3. Fichte gave these lectures in Berlin in the winter of 1807/08.
4. Fichte, "On the Publication of Same," from the foreword to *Die Anweisungen zum seligen Leben*, Berlin 1806.
5. Rudolf Steiner, "Understanding the Spiritual World (I)," lecture of April 18, 1914, pp. 1–17 in this volume.
6. Rudolf Steiner, *Four Mystery Plays,* (London: Rudolf Steiner Press, 1982). The four Mystery Dramas were premiered in Munich between 1910 and 1913 under Steiner's direction.
7. Steiner here refers to the actress Maria von Strauch-Spettini, 1847–1904. See Hella Wiesberger's short biography of Maria von Strauch-Spettini and her letters to Marie von Sivers in *Aus dem Leben von Marie Steiner-von Sivers,* Dornach 1956, p. 15ff.
8. Steiner here refers to Christian Morgenstern, May 6, 1871–March 31, 1914. German poet, wrote lyrical verse as well as grotesque and nonsense verse. Also translated works of Ibsen, Strindberg, and Hamsun.
9. Morgenstern, *Wir fanden einen Pfad.* ("We Found a Path"), first published by Piper Verlag, Munich, in autumn of 1914.
10. This lecture was given on December 31, 1913, as part of the lecture cycle *Christ and the Spiritual World: The Search for the Holy Grail* (London: Rudolf Steiner Press, 1963) at which Morgenstern was present. Rudolf Steiner's comments are in *Die*

Kunst der Rezitation und Deklamation, volume 281 in the Collected Works, (Dornach, Switzerland: Rudolf Steiner Verlag, 1967), pp. 208-210.

11. See Steiner, *Background to the Gospel of St. Mark,* (London: Rudolf Steiner Press, 1968), Lecture Six, pp. 96–113.

12. Raphael, 1483–1520, Italian painter.
Leonardo da Vinci, 1452–1519, Italian painter.

LECTURE THREE

1. Work on the construction of the first Goetheanum in Dornach. Started in 1913, it was destroyed by arson on New Year's Eve 1922/23.

2. Christian Morgenstern, May 6, 1871–March 31, 1914. See Lecture Two, note 8.

3. Christian Morgenstern, *Alles um des Menschen Willen: Briefe,* (Munich, Germany: Piper, 1962), letter of January 22, 1914, to a young girl, p. 398.

4. Morgenstern, *Wir fanden einen Pfad.* See Lecture Two, note 9.

5. Zarathustra, 628–551 B.C. Persian religious leader.
Buddha, Siddharta Gautama, 563–483 B.C. Founder of Buddhism.
Krishna, Indian deity, appears in Bhagavad-Gita as teacher of Arjuna.

6. Rudolf Steiner, "Homunkulus," public lecture, Berlin, March 26, 1914, in *Geisteswissenschaft als Lebensgut,* vol. 63 in the Collected Works, (Dornach, Switzerland: Rudolf Steiner Verlag, 1959).

LECTURE FOUR

1. See Rudolf Steiner, *Die Welt des Geistes und ihr Hereinragen in das physische Dasein,* vol. 150 in the Collected Works, (Dornach, Switzerland: Rudolf Steiner Verlag, 1972), lecture of May 5, 1913. There are no transcripts of the lectures of May 4 and 9, 1913, in Paris.

2. Rudolf Steiner, *Knowledge of the Higher Worlds and Its Attainment,* repr., (Hudson, NY: Anthroposophic Press, 1986).

3. Steiner here refers to the actress Maria von Strauch-Spettini, 1847–1904. See Lecture Two, note 7.
4. Edouard Schuré, French writer. His play *Children of Lucifer* was performed in German in Munich on August 22, 1909, under Rudolf Steiner's direction. See Steiner, *The East in the Light of the West* and Schuré, *Children of Lucifer*, both in one volume, (Blauvelt, NY: Spiritual Science Library, 1986).
5. Joan of Arc, 1412–1431, French national heroine and saint.
6. Morgenstern, see Lecture Two, note 8.
7. Due to complications and delays caused by World War I (1914-1918), the building neared completion only in 1920. The inauguration ceremony never took place because of the fire that destroyed the Goetheanum. A "provisional inauguration" took place on September 26, 1920, on the eve of the first event held in the building, the "first anthroposophical academic course," which lasted from September 27 to October 16, 1920.
8. Rudolf Steiner, *Vorstufen zum Mysterium von Golgatha*, vol. 152 in the Collected Works, (Dornach, Switzerland: Rudolf Steiner Verlag, 1964), Lecture of May 27, 1914.

LECTURE FIVE

1. At the beginning of this lecture, Rudolf Steiner apologized for giving the lecture in German rather than French. His comments were not recorded.
2. Nicolaus Copernicus, 1473–1543, Polish astronomer. Made astronomical observations of orbits of sun, moon, planets. Gradually abandoned accepted Ptolemaic system of astronomy and worked out heliocentric system.

Galileo Galilei, 1564–1642, Italian astronomer and physicist. Advocated Copernican system. Instrumental in laying foundations of modern science.

Giordano Bruno, 1548–1600, Italian philosopher. A critic of Aristotelian logic and defender of Copernican cosmology, which he extended with notion of infinite universe. Arrested and burned at the stake by the Inquisition.
3. Rudolf Steiner, *Knowledge of the Higher Worlds and Its Attainment*, repr., (Hudson, NY: Anthroposophic Press, 1986).

4. Steiner here refers to his investigation of events in the fourth century on the basis of spiritual science. He presented his insights in a lecture on May 9, 1914 ("Words of Remembrance for Oda Waller") in *Unsere Toten,* vol. 261 in the Collected Works, (Dornach, Switzerland: Rudolf Steiner Verlag, 1963); lecture on May 26, 1914 (Chapter Four, pp. 52–69 in this volume); lecture of March 23, 1921, in *Naturbeobachtung, Mathematik, wissenschaftliches Experiment und Erkenntnisergebnisse vom Gesichtspunkt der Anthroposophie,* vol. 324 in the Collected Works, (Dornach, Switzerland: Rudolf Steiner Verlag, 1972). He also mentioned these investigations and their results in his lecture on August 31, 1923, in *The Evolution of Consciousness,* (London: Pharos Books, 1979); and in his lecture on April 5, 1924, in *Karmic Relationships,* vol. 5, (London: Rudolf Steiner Press, 1966).
5. Steiner here refers to Oda Waller, sister of Mieta Pyle-Waller (who took the role of Johannes Thomasius in the Mystery Drama performances in Munich). See also his lecture of May 9, 1914, in *Unsere Toten.* Oda Waller died in March 1913.

LECTURE SIX

1. Lecture of April 16, 1914, entitled "Wie findet die Menschenseele ihre wahre Wesenheit?" ("How Can the Human Soul Find Its True Essence?").
2. Hermes, the ancient Greek herald and messenger of the gods. See also Lecture Three, note 5.
3. Max Müller, 1823–1900, German orientalist, linguist, and religious scholar, professor of philology at Oxford. Literally: "A change is to take place, a transformation of such magnitude that even if angels came down and announced it, we would understand it as little as an infant would understand what we told it about the world in our language," in *Leben und Religion* ("Life and Religion"), Stuttgart, n.y.

LECTURE SEVEN

1. Peter Rosegger, 1843–1918, Austrian poet and novelist.
   Hans Brandstetter, 1854–1925, Austrian sculptor.

Robert Hamerling, pseudonym of Rupert Hammerling, 1830–1889, Austrian poet. Best known for his epics *Ahasverus in Rom* (1865) and *Homunculus* (1888).

2. "An B(ertha)," Hamerling's last poem; written in the Stifting House on June 18, 1889, three weeks before his death. In *Letzte Grüsse aus Stiftinghaus,* in *Hamerlings Sämtliche Werke* (Hamerling's Collected Works), Leipzig 1893, 16 volumes, edited by Michael Rabenlechner, vol. 15, p. 90.

3. "The Pessimist" in *Letzte Grüsse aus Stiftinghaus,* p. 91. Translator's note: The final syllable of the German word "Pessimist" (*mist*) means "dung" in English.

4. Letter of June 11, 1888, in Peter Rosegger, *Persönliche Erinnerungen an Robert Hamerling,* Vienna 1891, p. 177.

5. Hamerling's philosophical work, published in 1891.

6. The Waldviertel is a region in northwestern Lower Austria.

7. Robert Hamerling, "Die schönste Gegend der Erde," vol. 16 in his Collected Works, p.134, and "Stationen meiner Lebenspilgerschaft," same volume, p. 17.

8. Jakob Böhme, 1575–1624. German mystic. He was first a shoemaker, then had a mystical experience in 1600.

9. Hamerling, "Stationen meiner Lebenspilgerschaft", p. 17.

10. "Stationen meiner Lebenspilgerschaft," p. 45.

11. "People still have the bad habit of asking me what I want to become — well, a human being!" from "Lehrjahre der Liebe," in *Tagebuchblätter und Briefe* (Diaries and Letters), entry of April 13, 1851. Volume 14 in Hamerling's Collected Works.

12. Literally: "The Greeks called the universe 'beauty' (cosmos)." In *Atomistik des Willens,* Hamburg 1891, vol. 11, p. 226.

13. In *Letzte Grüsse aus Stiftinghaus,* vol. 15 in Hamerling's Collected Works, pp. 34–35.

PUBLISHER'S NOTE

The lectures printed here were given by Rudolf Steiner to audiences familiar with the general background and terminology of his anthroposophical teaching. It should be remembered that in his autobiography *The Course of My Life,* he emphasizes the distinction between his written works on the one hand, and on the other, reports of lectures which were given as oral communications and were not originally intended for print. For an intelligent appreciation of the lectures it should be borne in mind that certain premises were taken for granted when the words were spoken. "These premises," Rudolf Steiner writes, "include at the very least the anthroposophical knowledge of Man and of the Cosmos in its spiritual essence; also what may be called 'anthroposophical history,' told as an outcome of research into the spiritual world."